FIND IT
in the
BIBLE

BOB PHILLIPS

is a marriage, family, and child counselor who has written more than seventy books, including *The Delicate Art of Dancing with Porcupines* and *Anger Is a Choice*. He has presented leadership seminars worldwide in nineteen countries and has appeared on a number of TV and radio programs across the United States. Bob and his wife of thirty-eight years live in south-central California and have two daughters and three grandsons.

Our purpose at Howard Publishing is to:

- *Increase faith* in the hearts of growing Christians
- *Inspire holiness* in the lives of believers
- *Instill hope* in the hearts of struggling people everywhere

Because He's coming again!

FIND IT IN THE BIBLE © 2004 by Bob Phillips
All rights reserved. Printed in the United States of America
Published by Howard Publishing Co., Inc.
3117 North 7th Street, West Monroe, Louisiana 71291-2227

Edited by Nancy Norris and Terry Whalin
Cover design by UDG | DesignWorks
Interior design by Stephanie D. Walker

Lists 17, 18, and 19 are from the *Bible Source Book* by Stephen D. Swihart, Victor Books, PO Box 1825, Wheaton, Illinois, 1977. Used by permission.

ISBN 0-7394-4712-2

CONTENTS

■CONTENTS

THE BIBLE

What book is that whose page divine
Bears God's impress on every line,
And in man's soul makes light to shine?
The Bible

When sin and sorrow, want and woe,
Assail poor mortals here below,
What book can then true comfort show?
The Bible

What paints the beautiful and true,
And mirrors at a single view
The paths which here we should pursue?
The Bible

What is the brightest gift the Lord
In his great mercy did award
To man, to be his shield and guard?
The Bible

What teaches love and truth and peace,
And bids good will 'mong men increase?
And bids strife, war and murder cease?
The Bible

Oh! What can make this world of woe
With peace and truth and virtue glow,
Till men no sin nor sorrow know?
The Bible

When error fled before its foes,
And Luther, like the morning, rose,
With what did he Rome's crimes expose?
The Bible

What is it now that baffles Rome,
Where error long has found a home,
In many a pagan pile and dome?
The Bible

What gives to man the power and will,
God's high behest to do fulfill
And points the way to Zion's hill?
The Bible

When death comes knocking at the door,
And man's short life on earth is o'er,
What tells of bliss for ever more?
The Bible

—Author Unknown

■LIST #1
5 Major Ways God Reveals Himself

Our eternal God uses 5 major methods to reveal Himself to mankind.

1. God Reveals Himself in Nature
   - God exists and has great glory.—Psalm 19:1–6
   - God is all powerful and will exercise judgment. —Romans 1:18–21

2. God Reveals Himself in Providential Care
   - God is kind to all people.—Matthew 5:45
   - God provides food for everyone.—Acts 14:15–17
   - God puts leaders in place and also removes them.—Daniel 2:21

3. God Reveals Himself through Man's Conscience
   - By right living the conscience does not reproach. —Job 27:6
   - God instructs all men with the law He placed in their hearts.—Romans 2:14–15

4. God Reveals Himself through Christ
   - Christ lets us know what the Father is like. —John 1:18
   - When you see Christ, you see the Father. —John 14:9
   - Christ lets us see His compassion.—Romans 9:15
   - God gives eternal life to all who will believe. —John 6:63; 14:10

5. God Reveals Himself through Scripture
   - God uses Scripture to give correction and guidance. —2 Timothy 3:16–17
   - God uses men to write the Scriptures guided by the Holy Spirit. —2 Peter 1:21

■LIST #2
26 Attributes of God

A study of God's characteristics will enrich our understanding of God.

1. God is all-knowing.—Hebrews 4:12–13

2. God is all-powerful.—Revelation 19:6

3. God is eternal.—Psalm 90:1–2

4. God is ever-present.—Psalm 139:7–12

5. God is faithful.—Psalm 46:1–2

6. God is father.—John 20:17

7. God is good.—Psalm 52:1

8. God is full of grace.—Ephesians 2:8–9

9. God is holy.—Leviticus 19:2

10. God is immense.—1 Kings 8:27

11. God is infinite.—Psalm 102:25–26

12. God is jealous.—Exodus 20:5

13. God is just.—Isaiah 45:21

14. God is full of kindness.—Psalm 36:7

15. God is long-suffering.—2 Peter 3:9

16. God is loving.—John 3:14–18

17. God is merciful.—2 Chronicles 30:9

18. God is patient.—Psalm 145:8

19. God is self-existent.—Exodus 3:14

20. God is sovereign.—Psalms 100:3; 103:19

21. God is spirit.—John 4:24

22. God is truth.—John 14:6

23. God is unchangeable.—Malachi 3:6; James 1:17

24. God is unity.—Deuteronomy 6:4

25. God is wisdom.—Romans 16:27

26. God is wrathful.—Romans 1:18

■LIST #3
18 Names of the Holy Spirit

The various names of the Holy Spirit provide helpful insight into this member of the deity.

1. Eternal Spirit—Hebrews 9:14

2. Holy One—1 John 2:20

3. Holy Spirit—Matthew 1:20

4. One Spirit—Ephesians 4:4

5. Seven Spirits—Revelation 1:4; 3:1

6. The Lord the Spirit—2 Corinthians 3:18

7. Spirit of Counsel—Isaiah 11:2

8. Spirit of Fear of the Lord—Isaiah 11:2

9. Spirit of Glory—1 Peter 4:14

10. Spirit of Grace—Hebrews 10:29

11. Spirit of Grace and Supplication—Zechariah 12:10

12. Spirit of Holiness—Romans 1:4

13. Spirit of Knowledge—Isaiah 11:2

14. Spirit of Life—Romans 8:2

15. Spirit of Might—Isaiah 11:2

16. Spirit of Truth—John 14:17

17. Spirit of Understanding—Isaiah 11:2

18. Spirit of Wisdom—Isaiah 11:2

▊LIST #4
31 Things God Hates

Use this list as a standard for your own life and also as a means of praying for individuals you know who participate in these actions.

1. God hates homosexual acts.—Leviticus 18:22

2. God hates sexual acts between humans and animals. —Leviticus 18:23

3. God hates blemished sacrifices.—Deuteronomy 17:1

4. God hates divination.—Deuteronomy 18:10

5. God hates astrology.—Deuteronomy 18:10

6. God hates enchanters.—Deuteronomy 18:10

7. God hates witches.—Deuteronomy 18:10

8. God hates charmers.—Deuteronomy 18:11

9. God hates wizards.—Deuteronomy 18:11

10. God hates necromancers.—Deuteronomy 18:11

11. God hates the workers of iniquity.—Psalm 5:5

12. God hates the wicked.—Psalm 11:5

13. God hates those who love violence.—Psalm 11:5

14. God hates a proud look.—Proverbs 6:16–17

15. God hates a lying tongue.—Proverbs 6:17

16. God hates hands that shed innocent blood. —Proverbs 6:17

17. God hates a heart that devises wicked imaginations.—Proverbs 6:18

18. God hates feet that are swift in running to mischief. —Proverbs 6:18

19. God hates a false witness who speaks lies. —Proverbs 6:19

20. God hates anyone who sows discord among brethren.—Proverbs 6:19

21. God hates lying lips.—Proverbs 12:22

22. God hates the thoughts of the wicked. —Proverbs 15:26

23. God hates the ways of the wicked.—Proverbs 15:9

24. God hates the proud in heart.—Proverbs 16:5

25. God hates those who justify the wicked. —Proverbs 17:15

26. God hates those who condemn the just. —Proverbs 17:15

27. God hates meaningless sacrifices.—Isaiah 1:13

28. God hates idolatry.—Jeremiah 44:2–4

29. God hates evil plans against neighbors. —Zechariah 8:17

30. God hates false oaths.—Zechariah 8:17

31. God hates divorce.—Malachi 2:14–16

LIST #5
7 Keys to Theology

Theology is the study of God and His relationship to the world. These passages provide a basic overview of biblical doctrines.

1. The Holy Scriptures

   - God's Written Revelation to Man
       John 7:17; 16:12–15
       1 Corinthians 2:7–14
       1 Thessalonians 2:13
       1 Timothy 3:15–17
       Hebrews 4:12
       2 Peter 1:20–21

2. God

   - One True God
       Deuteronomy 6:4
       Isaiah 45:5–7
       1 Corinthians 8:4
   - God the Father
       Psalm 145:8–9
       Romans 11:36
       1 Corinthians 8:6
       Ephesians 1:4–6; 3:9; 4:6
   - God the Son
       John 1:3; 10:30; 14:9
       Philippians 2:5–8
       Colossians 1:15–17; 2:9
       Hebrews 1:2

- God the Holy Spirit
    Psalm 139:7–10
    John 14:16–17; 15:26
    1 Corinthians 2:10–13
    Ephesians 4:30
    1 Corinthians 12:11
    Hebrews 9:14; 10:15–17

3. Man

- Man Created in God's Image
    Genesis 2:7; 15–25
    Isaiah 43:7
    Colossians 1:16
    James 3:9
    Revelation 4:11

4. Salvation

- Deliverance from Sin
    John 1:12
    Ephesians 1:4–7; 2:8–10
    1 Peter 1:18–19

- Election [Chosen by God]
    Romans 8:28–30
    Ephesians 1:4–11
    2 Thessalonians 2:13
    2 Timothy 2:10
    1 Peter 1:1–2

- Regeneration [Being Born Again]
    John 3:3–8; 5:24
    1 Corinthians 6:19–20
    Ephesians 5:17–21
    Colossians 3:12–17
    Titus 3:5
    2 Peter 1:4–11

11

- Justification [Being Made Right]
    Romans 2:4; 3:20; 8:30, 33
    2 Corinthians 7:10
    Colossians 2:14
    1 Peter 2:24

- Sanctification [Purity and Holy Living]
    Acts 20:32
    1 Corinthians 1:2, 30; 6:11
    2 Thessalonians 2:13
    Hebrews 2:11; 10:10, 14
    1 Peter 1:2

- Security [Assurance of Salvation]
    John 5:24; 6:37–40; 10:27–30
    Romans 5:9–10; 8:31–39
    Ephesians 4:30
    Hebrews 13:5

- Separation [Set Apart for God]
    Romans 12:1–2
    1 Corinthians 5:9–13; 6:14–7:1
    2 Timothy 3:1–5
    1 John 2:15–17

- Propitiation [God Is Satisfied]
    Romans 3:25
    Romans 5:11
    Hebrews 2:17
    1 John 2:2; 4:10

- Redemption [Purchased from Sin]
    John 1:29
    1 Timothy 4:10
    Titus 2:11
    2 Peter 3:9

- Repentance [Walking a New Direction]
    - Jeremiah 31:18–19
    - Mark 1:15
    - John 1:12; 5:24
    - Acts 5:31; 11:18
    - 2 Timothy 2:25
    - 2 Peter 1:1

5. The Church

- The Body of Christ
    - 1 Corinthians 12:12–13
    - 2 Corinthians 11:2
    - Ephesians 1:22; 5:23–32
    - Colossians 1:18
    - Revelation 19:7–8

6. Angels

- Holy Angels
    - Luke 2:9–14
    - Hebrews 1:6–7, 14; 2:6–7
    - Revelation 5:11–14

- Fallen Angels
    - Isaiah 14:12–17
    - Ezekiel 28:11–19
    - Matthew 25:41
    - Revelation 12:1–14

7. Last Things

- Death
    - Luke 23:43
    - 2 Corinthians 5:8
    - Philippians 1:23
    - James 2:26
    - Revelation 6:9–11

- Rapture of Church
    John 14:1–3
    1 Corinthians 15:51–53
    1 Thessalonians 4:15–5:11
    Titus 2:13

- Tribulation Period
    2 Thessalonians 2:7–12
    Revelation 16

- Second Coming / Millennial Reign
    Matthew 25:31
    Luke 1:32–33
    Acts 1:10–11; 2:29–30
    Revelation 19:11–16; 20:1–7

- Judgment of Lost
    Matthew 25:41
    John 5:22, 28–29
    Revelation 20:7–15

- Eternity
    2 Thessalonians 1:9
    2 Peter 3:10
    Revelation 20:7–15; 21:2

LIST #6
59 Names of Christ

The many distinct names used to refer to the Lord Jesus Christ provide insight into who He is.

1. Adam [the second] — 1 Corinthians 15:45

2. Advocate — 1 John 2:1

3. Alpha and Omega — Revelation 1:8; 22:13

4. Amen — Revelation 3:14

5. Angel of the Lord — Exodus 3:2; Judges 13:15–18

6. Branch — Jeremiah 23:5

7. Bread of Life — John 6:35, 48

8. Chief Cornerstone — Ephesians 2:20; 1 Peter 2:6

9. Chief Shepherd — 1 Peter 5:4

10. Counselor — Isaiah 9:6

11. Dayspring — Luke 1:78

12. Deliverer — Romans 11:26

13. Door — John 10:7

14. Immanuel — Isaiah 7:14; Matthew 1:23

15. Eternal Life — 1 John 1:2; 5:20

16. Everlasting Father — Isaiah 9:6

17. Faithful Witness — Revelation 1:5; 3:14

18. First and Last—Revelation 1:17; 2:8

19. God—Isaiah 40:9; John 20:28

20. Good Shepherd—John 10:14

21. Great High Priest—Hebrews 4:14

22. Holy One—Psalm 16:10; Acts 2:27; 3:14

23. I Am—Exodus 3:14; John 8:58

24. Jehovah—Isaiah 26:4 (KJV)

25. Jesus—Matthew 1:21; 1 Thessalonians 1:10

26. Just One—Acts 7:52

27. King—Zechariah 9:9; Matthew 21:5

28. Lamb of God—John 1:29, 36

29. Life—John 14:6; Colossians 3:4

30. Light of the World—John 8:12

31. Lion of Judah—Revelation 5:5

32. Lord God Almighty—Revelation 15:3

33. Lord of Glory—1 Corinthians 2:8

34. Messiah—Daniel 9:25; John 1:41

35. Mighty God—Isaiah 9:6

36. Morning Star—Revelation 22:16

37. Nazarene—Matthew 2:23

38. Our Passover—1 Corinthians 5:7

39. Prince of Life—Acts 3:15

40. Prince of Peace—Isaiah 9:6

41. Prophet—Luke 24:19; John 7:40

42. Redeemer—Isaiah 59:20; 60:16

43. Resurrection and Life—John 11:25

44. Rock—1 Corinthians 10:4

45. Savior—2 Peter 2:20; 3:18

46. Servant—Isaiah 42:1; 52:13

47. Son of God—Luke 1:35; John 1:49

48. Son of Man—John 5:27; 6:27

49. Sun of Righteousness—Malachi 4:2

50. True God—1 John 5:20

51. True Light—John 1:9

52. True Vine—John 15:1

53. Truth—John 14:6

54. Way—John 14:6

55. Witness—Isaiah 55:4

56. Wonderful—Isaiah 28:29; 9:6

57. Word—John 1:1

58. Word of God—Revelation 19:13

59. Word of Life—1 John 1:1

◣LIST #7
39 Parables of Jesus

Jesus captured the imagination of people through telling parables.

1. The Candle under a Bushel—Matthew 5:14–16

2. The House on Rock and Sand—Matthew 7:24–27

3. The New Cloth and Old Garment—Matthew 9:16

4. The New Wine in Old Wine Skins—Matthew 9:17

5. The Seed Sower—Matthew 13:3–23

6. The Tares—Matthew 13:24–30

7. The Mustard Seed—Matthew 13:31–32

8. The Hidden Treasure—Matthew 13:44

9. The Pearl—Matthew 13:45–46

10. The Fish Net—Matthew 13:47–50

11. The Lost Sheep—Matthew 18:12–14

12. The Unmerciful Servant—Matthew 18:23–35

13. The Laborers in the Vineyard—Matthew 20:1–16

14. The Two Sons—Matthew 21:28–32

15. The Vineyard—Matthew 21:33–44

16. The Marriage Feast—Matthew 22:2–14

17. The Fig Tree—Matthew 24:32–44

18. The Ten Virgins—Matthew 25:1–13

19. The Talents—Matthew 25:14–30

20. The Growing Seed—Mark 4:26–29

21. The Master Takes a Far Journey—Mark 13:34–37

22. The Two Debtors—Luke 7:41–43

23. The Good Samaritan—Luke 10:30–37

24. The Persistent Friend—Luke 11:5–13

25. The Rich Fool—Luke 12:16–21

26. The Wise Stewards—Luke 12:37–48

27. The Barren Fig Tree—Luke 13:6–9

28. The Leaven—Luke 13:20–21

29. The Great Supper—Luke 14:16–24

30. The Unfinished Tower—Luke 14:28–30

31. The King Goes to War—Luke 14:31–33

32. The Lost Coin—Luke 15:8–10

33. The Prodigal Son—Luke 15:11–32

34. The Unjust Steward—Luke 16:1–13

35. The Rich Man and Lazarus—Luke 16:19–31

36. The Unworthy Servants—Luke 17:7–10

37. The Persistent Woman—Luke 18:1–8

38. The Pharisee and the Publican—Luke 18:9–14

39. The Pounds of Reward—Luke 19:11–27

LIST #8
37 Miracles Performed by Jesus

Throughout His ministry, Jesus demonstrated His divine nature through miracles. This list celebrates God's miraculous touch on humankind.

1. A leper is cleansed.—Matthew 8:2–3
2. A centurion's servant is healed.—Matthew 8:5–13
3. Peter's mother-in-law is cured.—Matthew 8:14–15
4. The sick are healed.—Matthew 8:16
5. He calms the storm.—Matthew 8:23–27
6. Two men are cured of demons.—Matthew 8:28–32
7. A paralytic is healed.—Matthew 9:2–7
8. The ruler's daughter is raised form the dead. —Matthew 9:18–25
9. A woman with a blood disease is healed. —Matthew 9:20–22
10. Two blind men are healed.—Matthew 9:27–31
11. A deaf, demon-possessed man is cured. —Matthew 9:32–33
12. A withered hand is healed.—Matthew 12:9–13
13. A blind, mute, demon-possessed man is healed. —Matthew 12:22
14. More than 5,000 people are fed.—Matthew 14:16–21
15. Jesus walks on the water.—Matthew 14:25
16. A Gentile woman's daughter is healed. —Matthew 15:22–28

17. More than 4,000 people are fed.
    —Matthew 15:32–38

18. An epileptic boy is cured.—Matthew 17:14–18

19. Tax money is found in a fish's mouth.
    —Matthew 17:24–27

20. Two blind men are healed.—Matthew 20:30–34

21. A fig tree is cursed.—Matthew 21:18–19

22. An unclean spirit is cast out.—Mark 1:23

23. A deaf mute is cured.—Mark 7:31–35

24. A blind man is healed.—Mark 8:22–25

25. Jesus escapes from a hostile crowd.—Luke 4:28–30

26. Fish are caught in astounding numbers.—Luke 5:4–7

27. A widow's son is raised from the dead.—Luke 7:11–15

28. A woman with a bent back is cured.—Luke 13:11–13

29. A man with dropsy is healed.—Luke 14:1–4

30. Ten lepers are cleansed.—Luke 17:11–19

31. A servant's ear is restored.—Luke 22:51

32. Water is turned into wine.—John 2:1–10

33. A nobleman's son is healed.—John 4:46–53

34. A crippled man is healed at Bethesda.—John 5:1–9

35. A man, blind from birth, is cured.—John 9:1–12

36. Lazarus is raised from the dead.—John 11:38–44

37. Jesus provides an incredible catch of fish.
    —John 21:4–6

■ LIST #9

25 Old Testament Prophecies Fulfilled by Jesus

These amazing prophecies and their fulfillment inspire faith in God's overarching plan.

Old Testament Prophecies	New Testament Fulfillments
1. His soul would not stay in hell. —Psalm 16:10	Acts 2:24
2. He would cry out on the cross. —Psalm 22:1	Matthew 27:46
3. He would be ridiculed on the cross. —Psalm 22:7–8	Matthew 27:39–40
4. Christ's garments would be divided. —Psalm 22:18	Matthew 27:35
5. His bones would not be broken. —Psalm 34:20	John 19:30–36
6. He would be betrayed by a friend. —Psalm 41:9	John 13:18–30
7. Gifts would be given. —Psalm 68:18	Ephesians 4:7
8. He would be hated by many. —Psalm 69:4	John 15:24–25
9. He would be thirsty. —Psalm 69:21	John 19:28–29
10. He would speak in parables. —Psalm 78:2	Matthew 13:34–35
11. People would not understand Him. —Isaiah 6:9	Matthew 13:13–14

12. People would not believe Him.
    —Isaiah 6:10 ....John 12:39–41

13. He would be born of a virgin.
    —Isaiah 7:14 ....Matthew 1:18–25

14. He had to leave the land.
    —Isaiah 9:1–2 ....Matthew 4:12–16

15. He would not promote Himself.
    —Isaiah 42:1–3 ....Matthew 12:14–21

16. He would be rejected by men.
    —Isaiah 53:3 ....Luke 9:22

17. He would bear our sicknesses.
    —Isaiah 53:4 ....Matthew 8:16–17

18. He would die with thieves.
    —Isaiah 53:9 ....Matthew 27:38

19. He would be buried with the wealthy.
    —Isaiah 53:9 ....Mark 15:43

20. He would fulfill Scripture.
    —Isaiah 61:1–2 ....Luke 4:16–21

21. He would be called out of Egypt.
    —Hosea 11:1 ....Matthew 2:13–15

22. He would be born in Bethlehem.
    —Micah 5:2 ....Matthew 2:1, 5–6

23. He would ride into Jerusalem on a donkey.
    —Zechariah 9:9 ....Matthew 21:1–11

24. 30 silver pieces would buy His betrayal.
    —Zechariah 11:12–13 ....Matthew 27:3–10

25. He would be pierced.
    —Zechariah 12:10 ....John 19:34, 37

LIST #10
The 6 Trials of Jesus

Most people believe Jesus was subjected to only one trial, but the Gospels point out that Jesus endured 6 distinct trials.

1. Before Annas—John 18:12–24

2. Before Caiaphas—Matthew 26:57–58; Mark 14:53–65

3. Before Chief Priests and Elders—Matthew 27:1–2; Mark 15:1; Luke 22:66–71

4. Before Pontius Pilate—Matthew 27:11–14; Mark 15:1–5; Luke 23:1–7; John 18:28–38

5. Before Herod—Luke 23:8–12

6. Before Pontius Pilate—Matthew 27:15–26; Mark 15:6–15; Luke 23:18–25; John 18:29–19:16

■ LIST #11
7 Last Sayings of Jesus on the Cross

These are the final words Jesus uttered before His death on the cross for the sins of the world.

1. Then Jesus said, "Father, forgive them, for they do not know what they do."—Luke 23:34

2. And Jesus said to him, [the thief on the cross] "Assuredly, I say to you, today you will be with Me in Paradise."—Luke 23:43

3. He said to His mother, "Woman, behold your son!" Then He said to the disciple, "Behold your mother!" —John 19:26–27

4. Jesus cried out with a loud voice, saying, "Eloi, Eloi, lama sabachthani?" which is translated, "My God, My God, why have You forsaken Me?"—Mark 15:34

5. After this, Jesus, knowing that all things were now accomplished, that the Scripture might be fulfilled, said, "I thirst!"—John 19:28

6. So when Jesus had received the sour wine, He said, "It is finished!"—John 19:30

7. And when Jesus had cried out with a loud voice, He said, "Father, into Your hands I commit My spirit!" Having said this, He breathed His last.—Luke 23:46

■LIST #12
7 Great "I Ams" of Jesus

The religious leaders of Jesus's day were confounded and confused with His "I Am" statements, which proclaimed His equality with God.

1. I am the bread of life.—John 6:35

2. I am the light of the world.—John 8:12

3. I am the door.—John 10:9

4. I am the good shepherd.—John 10:11

5. I am the resurrection and the life.—John 11:25

6. I am the way, the truth, and the life.—John 14:6

7. I am the vine.—John 15:1, 5

LIST #13
18 More "I Ams" of Jesus

The following list of 18 "I Ams" of Jesus Christ have profound implications.

1. I am willing.—Matthew 8:3
2. I am sending you.—Matthew 10:16; John 20:21
3. I am gentle.—Matthew 11:29
4. I am.—Mark 14:61–62; Matthew 27:43; Luke 22:70; John 10:36
5. I am with you always.—Matthew 28:20
6. I am among you.—Luke 22:27
7. I am from above.—John 8:23
8. Before Abraham was . . . I AM.—John 8:58
9. I am lifted up.—John 12:32
10. Teacher and Lord . . . I am.—John 13:13
11. I am in the Father.—John 14:11
12. I am a king.—John 18:37
13. I am the Alpha and Omega.—Revelation 1:8
14. I am the First and the Last.—Revelation 1:17
15. I am He who lives.—Revelation 1:18
16. Here I am! I stand and knock.—Revelation 3:20 (NIV)
17. I am the Root and Offspring of David.—Revelation 22:16
18. I am coming quickly.—Revelation 22:20

▄LIST #14

20 Instructions for Awaiting Christ's Return

Throughout the ages, Christians have waited with great anticipation and expectation for the return of Jesus Christ. This list provides encouragement to believers.

1. Watch. — Matthew 24:42–44; 25:13; Mark 13:32–37

2. Be sober. — 1 Thessalonians 5:2–6; 1 Peter 1:13; 4:7

3. Repent. — Acts 3:19–21; Revelation 3:3

4. Be faithful. — Matthew 25:19–21; Luke 12:42–44

5. Be proud of Christ. — Mark 8:38

6. Guard against worldliness. — Matthew 16:26–27

7. Be gentle. — Philippians 4:5

8. Be patient. — I Thessalonians 5:14; James 5:7

9. Put away fleshly desires. — Colossians 3:3–5; Titus 2:11–13

10. Be sincere. — Philippians 1:9–10

11. Be holy before God. — 1 Thessalonians 5:23; 1 Peter 1:15–16

12. Be faithful as a minister. — 2 Timothy 4:1–2; 1 Peter 5:2–4

13. Be pure. — John 3:2–3

14. Abide in Christ. — 1 John 2:28

15. Endure testings. — 1 Peter 1:7

16. Show love. — 1 Thessalonians 3:12–13

17. Receive citizenship in heaven. — Philippians 3:20–21

18. Look for Christ. — 2 Timothy 4:7–8; Hebrews 9:27–28

19. Have confidence in Christ. — Philippians 1:6

20. Guard against hasty judgment. — 1 Corinthians 4:5

◼️ LIST #15
Christ in Every Book of the Bible

While the word *Christ* doesn't appear in every book of the Bible, the foreshadowing and presence of Jesus is present throughout each book of Scripture.

In Genesis Christ is the Seed of the Woman.

In Exodus Christ is the Passover Lamb.

In Leviticus Christ is our High Priest.

In Numbers Christ is the Pillar of Cloud by day and the Pillar of Fire by night.

In Deuteronomy Christ is the Prophet like unto Moses.

In Joshua Christ is the Captain of our Salvation.

In Judges Christ is our Judge and Lawgiver.

In Ruth Christ is our Kinsman-Redeemer.

In Samuel Christ is our Trusted Prophet.

In Kings and Chronicles Christ is our Reigning King.

In Ezra and Nehemiah Christ is the Rebuilder of the broken-down walls of human life.

In Nehemiah Christ is the rebuilder.

In Esther Christ is our Mordecai.

In Job Christ is our Ever-Living Redeemer: for I know my redeemer lives.

In Psalms Christ is our Shepherd.

In Proverbs and Ecclesiastes Christ is our Wisdom.

In the Song of Solomon Christ is our Lover and Bridegroom.

In Isaiah Christ is the Prince of Peace.

In Jeremiah Christ is the Righteous Branch.

In Lamentations Christ is our Weeping Prophet.

In Ezekiel Christ is the wonderful Four-Faced Man.

And in Daniel Christ is the Fourth Man in "Life's Fiery Furnaces."

In Hosea Christ is the Faithful Husband, "Forever married to the backslider."

In Joel Christ is the Baptizer with the Holy Ghost and Fire.

In Amos Christ is our Burden-Bearer.

In Obadiah Christ is the Mighty to Save.

In Jonah Christ is our great Foreign Missionary.

In Micah Christ is the Messenger of Beautiful Feet.

In Nahum Christ is the Avenger of God's Elect.

In Habakkuk Christ is God's Evangelist, crying, "Revive your work in the midst of the years."

In Zephaniah Christ is our Savior.

In Haggai Christ is the Restorer of God's lost heritage.

In Zechariah Christ is the Fountain opened to the house of David for sin and uncleanness.

Malachi Christ is the Sun of Righteousness, rising with healing in His wings.

In Matthew Christ is the Messiah.

In Mark Christ is the Wonder-Worker.

In Luke Christ is the Son of Man.

In John Christ is the Son of God.

In Acts Christ is the Holy Ghost.

In Romans Christ is our Justifier.

In Corinthians Christ is our Sanctifier.

In Galatians Christ is our Redeemer from the curse of the law.

In Ephesians Christ is the Christ of unsearchable riches.

In Philippians Christ is the God who supplies all our needs.

In Colossians Christ is the fullness of the Godhead, bodily.

In Thessalonians Christ is our Soon-Coming King.

In Timothy Christ is our Mediator between God and man.

In Titus Christ is our Faithful Pastor.

In Philemon Christ is a Friend that sticketh closer than a brother.

In Hebrews Christ is the Blood of the Everlasting Covenant.

In James Christ is our Great Physician, for "The prayer of faith shall save the sick."

In Peter Christ is our Chief Shepherd, who soon shall appear with a crown of unfading glory.

In John Christ is Love.

In Jude Christ is the Lord coming with ten thousands of His saints.

And in Revelation Christ is the King of kings and Lord of lords!

LIST #16
22 Names for Scripture

Throughout the Bible, different terms or words are used for the Bible. Each one is significant.

1. The Scripture—Mark 12:10

2. The Scriptures—Matthew 21:42

3. The Holy Scriptures—Romans 1:2

4. The Oracles of God—Romans 3:2

5. The Law of Moses and the Prophets and the Psalms —Luke 24:44

6. The Word of God—Mark 7:13

7. The Word of Christ—Colossians 3:16

8. The Sword of the Spirit—Ephesians 6:17

9. The Word of Life—Philippians 2:16

10. The Word of Truth—Proverbs 22:21

11. The Scripture of Truth—Daniel 10:21

12. The Word of the Gospel—Acts 15:7

13. The Word of Truth—Ephesians 1:13

14. The Word of the Lord—1 Thessalonians 4:15

15. The Word of Reconciliation—2 Corinthians 5:19

16. The Covenants, the Law, and the Promises —Romans 9:4

17. His Testimonies—Psalm 119:2

18. The Old and New Covenant—Hebrews 9:15

19. His Precepts—Psalm 119:40

20. His Commandments—Psalm 119:6

21. His Statutes—Psalm 119:5

22. The Law—Matthew 12:5

LIST #17
Who Wrote the Old Testament and When

Name of Book	Author	Estimated Date of Writing
Pentateuch		
Genesis	Moses	1445 BC
Exodus	Moses	1444 BC
Leviticus	Moses	1443 BC
Numbers	Moses	1443–1405 BC
Deuteronomy	Moses	1405 BC
Conquest and Monarchy		
Joshua	Joshua	1375 BC
Judges	Samuel	1375–1075 BC
Ruth	Samuel	During the Judges
1 Samuel	Unknown	1000 BC
2 Samuel	Unknown	960 BC
1 Kings	Unknown	Sixth Century BC
2 Kings	Unknown	Sixth Century BC
1 Chronicles	Ezra	Fifth Century BC
2 Chronicles	Ezra	Fifth Century BC
Post-Exilic Events		
Ezra	Ezra	535–475 BC
Nehemiah	Ezra	445–433 BC
Esther	Unknown	483–474 BC

Poetry

Job	Unknown	1800 BC
Psalms	Several Authors	1440–580 BC
Proverbs	Solomon and Others	950 BC
Ecclesiastes	Solomon	935 BC
Song of Solomon	Solomon	960 BC

Prophets

Isaiah	Isaiah	739–700 BC
Jeremiah	Jeremiah	627–560 BC
Lamentations	Jeremiah	586 BC
Ezekiel	Ezekiel	593–571 BC
Daniel	Daniel	606–534 BC
Hosea	Hosea	760–725 BC
Joel	Joel	838 BC
Amos	Amos	760 BC
Obadiah	Unknown	845 BC
Jonah	Jonah	782 BC
Micah	Micah	735 BC
Nahum	Nahum	650 BC
Habakkuk	Habakkuk	609–599 BC
Zephaniah	Zephaniah	640 BC
Haggai	Haggai	520 BC
Zechariah	Zechariah	520 BC
Malachi	Malachi	500 BC

LIST #18
Who Wrote the New Testament and When

Name of Book	Author	Estimated Date of Writing
Biography		
Matthew	Matthew	AD 60
Mark	Mark	AD 60
Luke	Luke	AD 60
John	John	AD 60
History		
Acts	Luke	AD 64
Letters		
Romans	Paul	AD 58
1 Corinthians	Paul	AD 56
2 Corinthians	Paul	AD 57
Galatians	Paul	AD 56
Ephesians	Paul	AD 62
Philippians	Paul	AD 62
Colossians	Paul	AD 62
1 Thessalonians	Paul	AD 52
2 Thessalonians	Paul	AD 52
1 Timothy	Paul	AD 64
2 Timothy	Paul	AD 66
Titus	Paul	AD 64

Philemon	Paul	AD 62
Hebrews	Unknown	AD 70
James	James	AD 60
1 Peter	Peter	AD 63
2 Peter	Peter	AD 68
1 John	John	AD 85–90
2 John	John	AD 85–90
3 John	John	AD 85–90
Jude	Jude	AD 65–80

Prophecy

Revelation	John	AD 90–96

LIST #19
66 Individual Book Themes

Capture the theme of the Bible in a single word or phrase? This list will give you an overview of the entire Bible.

1. Genesis—Beginnings

2. Exodus—Redemption through Blood

3. Leviticus—Holiness through Sacrifice

4. Numbers—Wilderness Trials

5. Deuteronomy—Preparations for Entering the Promised Land

6. Joshua—Possessing the Inheritance

7. Judges—Judges for Repentant Israel

8. Ruth—Kinsman-Redeemer

9. 1 Samuel—The Monarchy Begins

10. 2 Samuel—David, Israel's Greatest King

11. 1 Kings—The Monarchy Is Divided

12. 2 Kings—The Fall of Israel and Judah

13. 1 Chronicles—David—Israel's Greatest King

14. 2 Chronicles—The House of God and Judah's Fall

15. Ezra—Returning to Jerusalem

16. Nehemiah—Rebuilding Jerusalem

17. Esther—A Threat to Israel

18. Job—The Mystery of Why the Righteous Suffer

19. Psalms—Praise

20. Proverbs—Wisdom through Instruction

21. Ecclesiastes—A Sermon on Vanity

22. Song of Solomon—A Love Affair

23. Isaiah—Salvation through God's Servant

24. Jeremiah—Judgment of Israel's Monarchy

25. Lamentations—Sorrow over Jerusalem

26. Ezekiel—Consummation of Israel's Monarchy

27. Daniel—The Times of the Gentiles

28. Hosea—God's Covenantal Love

29. Joel—The Day of the Lord

30. Amos—God Judges Sin and Promises a Blessing

31. Obadiah—Retribution for Edom

32. Jonah—Jonah's Reluctance and Nineveh's Repentance

33. Micah—God Judges Sin and Promises a Blessing

34. Nahum—Judgment upon Nineveh

35. Habakkuk—The Just Shall Live by Faith

36. Zephaniah—The Day of the Lord

37. Haggai—Mandate to Rebuild the Temple—Rebuke

38. Zechariah—Mandate to Finish the Temple —Exhortation

39. Malachi—Rebuke for Lukewarm Worship

40. Matthew—Jesus, the Promised and Rejected Messiah

41. Mark—Jesus, the Perfect Servant of God

42. Luke—Jesus, the Perfect Man and Savior

43. John—Jesus, the Savior of the World

44. Acts—The Works of Jesus through the Church

45. Romans—Three Peoples: Gentiles, Jews, and the Church

46. 1 Corinthians—Answering Questions and Correcting Problems

47. 2 Corinthians—Paul's Ministry

48. Galatians—A Defense for Christian Liberty

49. Ephesians—The Believer's Position, Walk, and Warfare

50. Philippians—Rejoicing in Christ

51. Colossians—The Preeminence of Jesus Christ

52. 1 Thessalonians—The Second Coming of Christ

53. 2 Thessalonians—The Second Coming of Christ

54. 1 Timothy—Proper Order in the Church

55. 2 Timothy—Exhortations to Pastors

56. Titus—The Character of the Saint

57. Philemon—Paul's Entreaty for Onesimus

58. Hebrews—Jesus: Our Great Savior and Priest

59. James—Faith and Works Are Inseparable

60. 1 Peter—Encouragement for Perils from Without

61. 2 Peter—Exhortations for Perils from Within

62. 1 John—Fellowship with God and One Another

63. 2 John—Exhortations to Love and to Beware

64. 3 John—Compliments and Exhortations Regarding Conduct

65. Jude—Contending for the Faith

66. Revelation—The Unveiling of Jesus Christ and Last Things

LIST #20
135 Bible Characters and the Meaning of Their Names

The Scriptures are filled with stories about people. Here's a list of 135 Bible characters, the meaning of their names, and where to find them in the Word.

Name	Meaning	Reference
1. Aaron	Light	Exodus 4:14
2. Abed-nego	Servant or worshiper of Nebo	Daniel 1:7
3. Abel	Vanity	Genesis 4:2
4. Abihu	He is my father	Exodus 6:23
5. Abijah	Of Jehovah	1 Kings 14:1
6. Abner	Father of light	1 Samuel 14:50
7. Abraham	Father of a great multitude	Genesis 17:5
8. Absalom	Father of peace	2 Samuel 3:3
9. Achan	Troubler	Joshua 7:18
10. Adam	Red	Genesis 2:19
11. Adonijah	Jehovah is my Lord	2 Samuel 3:4
12. Agag	Flaming	Numbers 24:7
13. Ahab	Uncle	1 Kings 16:29
14. Ahaz	Possessor	2 Kings 15:38
15. Amos	Burden	Amos 1:1–2

Name	Meaning	Reference
16. Ananias	Jehovah has been gracious	Acts 5:1
17. Andrew	Manly	Mark 1:29
18. Annas	Gracious	Luke 3:2
19. Apollos	Mighty in Scripture	Acts 18:24
20. Apollyon	One that exterminates	Revelation 9:11
21. Aquila	an Eagle	Acts 18:2, 19
22. Asa	Physician	1 Kings 15:8
23. Asher	Fortunate, happy	Genesis 30:13
24. Balaam	Destruction	Numbers 22:5
25. Barabbas	Son of Abba	Mark 15:7
26. Barak	Thunderbolt, lightning	Judges 4:6
27. Barnabas	Son of encouragement	Acts 4:36
28. Bartholomew	Son of Talmai	Matthew 10:3
29. Bartimaeus	Son of Timaeus	Mark 10:46
30. Benaiah	Whom Jehovah has built	2 Samuel 23:20
31. Benjamin	Son of right hand	Genesis 35:18
32. Ben-Ammi	Son of my parents	Genesis 19:38
33. Boaz	Fleetness	Ruth 2–4
34. Caiaphas	Depression	John 11:49
35. Cain	Possession	Genesis 4:1
36. Caleb	A dog	Numbers 13:30

Name	Meaning	Reference
37. Cornelius	Of a horn	Acts 10:1
38. Dan	Judge	Genesis 30:6
39. Daniel	God's judge	Daniel 1:6
40. David	Beloved	1 Samuel 16:13
41. Deborah	Bee	Judges 4:4
42. Delilah	Delicate	Judges 16:4
43. Demas	Popular	Colossians 4:14
44. Dinah	Vindicated	Genesis 30:21
45. Dorcas	Gazelle	Acts 9:36
46. Eleazar	Whom God aids	Exodus 6:23
47. Eli	Height	1 Samuel 1:3
48. Elijah	My God is Jehovah	1 Kings 17:1
49. Eliphaz	To whom God is strength	Job 4:1
50. Elisha	To whom God is salvation	1 Kings 19:16
51. Elizabeth	God is my oath	Luke 1:5
52. Enoch	Experienced	Genesis 4:17
53. Ephraim	Fruitful	Genesis 41:52
54. Esau	Hairy	Genesis 25:25
55. Esther	Star	Esther 2:7
56. Eve	Life	Genesis 3:20
57. Ezekiel	Whom God will strengthen	Ezekiel 1:3

Name	Meaning	Reference
58. Ezra	Help	Ezra 7:1
59. Felix	Happy	Acts 23:24
60. Festus	Joyful	Acts 24:27
61. Gabriel	Man of God	Daniel 8:16
62. Gad	Good fortune	Genesis 30:11
63. Gamaliel	Benefit of God	Acts 5:34
64. Gideon	One who cuts down	Judges 6:11
65. Habakkuk	Embrace	Habakkuk 1:1
66. Hagar	Flight	Genesis 16:3
67. Haggai	Festive	Haggai 1:2
68. Ham	Warm	Genesis 9:18
69. Hannah	Gracious	1 Samuel 2:1
70. Herod	Sprung from a hero	Matthew 2:1
71. Hezekiah	The might of Jehovah	2 Kings 18:1
72. Hosea	Salvation	Hosea 1:1
73. Isaac	Laughter	Genesis 17:19
74. Isaiah	Salvation of Jehovah	Isaiah 1:1
75. Iscariot	Man of Kerioth	Matthew 10:4
76. Ishmael	Whom God hears	Genesis 16:15
77. Israel	Soldier with God	Genesis 32:28
78. Issachar	He is hired	Genesis 30:18
79. Jabez	Causing pain	1 Chronicles 4:9

Name	Meaning	Reference
80. Jacob	Supplanter	Genesis 25:26
81. James	Supplanter	James 1:1
82. Jehoshaphat	Whom Jehovah judges	1 Kings 15:24
83. Jeremiah	Whom Jehovah has appointed	Jeremiah 1:1
84. Jesse	Gift	Ruth 4:17
85. Jethro	Excellence	Exodus 3:1
86. Jezebel	Unmarried	1 Kings 16:31
87. Joab	Jehovah is father	2 Samuel 2:13
88. Job	One persecuted	Job 1:1
89. John	Jehovah is gracious	Matthew 3:1
90. Jonah	Dove	Jonah 1:1
91. Jonathan	Whom Jehovah gave	1 Samuel 13:2
92. Joseph	He shall add	Genesis 30:24
93. Joshua	Jehovah is salvation	Numbers 14:6
94. Judah	Praised	Genesis 29:35
95. Judas	Praised	Matthew 10:4
96. Mark	Large hammer	Acts 12:12
97. Mary	Rebellion	Matthew 1:16
98. Matthew	Gift of God	Matthew 9:9
99. Melchizedek	King of righteousness	Genesis 14:18
100. Methuselah	Man of the dart	Genesis 5:21

Name	Meaning	Reference
101. Micah	Who is like unto Jehovah	Micah 1:1
102. Michael	Who is like unto God	Jude 1:9
103. Miriam	Rebellion	Exodus 15:20
104. Mordecai	Consecrated to Merodach	Esther 2:5
105. Moses	Saved from the water	Exodus 2:10
106. Naphtali	My wrestling	Genesis 30:8
107. Nathan	Gift	2 Samuel 7:2
108. Nehemiah	Jehovah comforts	Nehemiah 1:1
109. Nicodemus	Victor over the people	John 3:1
110. Noah	Rest	Genesis 5:29
111. Obadiah	Worshiper of Jehovah	Obadiah 1:1
112. Paul	Little	Acts 13:9
113. Peter	A stone	Matthew 16:18
114. Pharaoh	The sun	Genesis 12:14
115. Philemon	Affectionate	Philemon 1:1
116. Philip	Lover of horses	John 1:43
117. Priscilla	Diminutive	Acts 18:2
118. Rachel	Ewe	Genesis 29:6
119. Rahab	Broad	Joshua 2:1
120. Rebekah	A noose	Genesis 22:23
121. Reuben	Behold a son	Genesis 29:31
122. Ruth	Friendship	Ruth 1:4

FIND IT IN THE BIBLE

Name	Meaning	Reference
123. Samuel	Name of God	1 Samuel 1:20
124. Sarah	Princess	Genesis 17:15
125. Satan	Accuser	1 Chronicles 21:1
126. Saul	Asked for	1 Samuel 9:2
127. Seth	Substitute	Genesis 4:25
128. Shadrach	Command of Aku	Daniel 1:7
129. Silas	Of the forest	Acts 15:22
130. Simon	Hearing	Matthew 13:55
131. Solomon	Peaceable	2 Samuel 5:14
132. Tamar	A palm tree	Genesis 38:6
133. Timothy	Honoring God	Acts 16:1
134. Zacharias	Whom Jehovah remembers	Luke 1:5
135. Zechariah	Whom Jehovah remembers	2 Kings 14:29

LIST #21
43 Kings of Israel and Judah

This list captures the predominant character traits of the kings of Israel and Judah and will help you understand the big picture of these kings in Jewish history.

The United Kingdom

King	Type of King	Years Reigned	Prophets	Scripture
1. Saul	Bad	40	Samuel	1 Samuel 9–31
2. David	Godly	40	Nathan	2 Samuel
3. Solomon	Mixed	40		1 Kings 2–11

The Northern Kingdom of Israel

King	Type of King	Years Reigned	Prophets	Scripture
4. Jeroboam I	Evil	22		1 Kings 12–14

King	Type of King	Years Reigned	Prophets	Scripture
5. Nadab	Evil	2		1 Kings 15
6. Baasha	Evil	24		1 Kings 15–16
7. Elah	Evil	2		1 Kings 16
8. Zimri	Evil	7 Days		1 Kings 16
9. Tibni	Evil	Does not say		1 Kings 16
10. Omri	Evil	12		1 Kings 16
11. Ahab	Evil	22	Elijah	1 Kings 16–22
12. Ahaziah	Evil	2	Elijah	2 Kings 8–9, 22
13. Jehoram	Evil	12	Elisha	2 Kings 2–8
14. Jehu	Mixed	28	Elisha	2 Kings 9–10
15. Jehoahaz	Evil	17	Elisha	2 Kings 13
16. Jehoash	Good	40	Elisha	2 Kings 12
17. Jeroboam II	Evil	41	Jonah, Amos	1 Kings 11–15
18. Zechariah	Evil	6 Months	Hosea	2 Kings 15
19. Shallum	Evil	1 Month	Hosea	2 Kings 15
20. Menahem	Evil	10	Hosea	2 Kings 15

21. Pekahiah	Evil	2	Hosea	2 Kings 15
22. Pekah	Evil	20	Hosea	2 Kings 15
23. Hoshea	Evil	9	Hosea	2 Kings 15, 17

The Southern Kingdom of Judah

King	Type of King	Years Reigned	Prophets	Scripture
24. Rehoboam	Evil	17		1 Kings 12–14, 2 Chronicles 10–12
25. Abijah	Evil	3		1 Kings 15, 2 Chronicles 13
26. Asa	Godly	5		1 Kings 15, 2 Chronicles 14–16
27. Jehoshaphat	Godly	25		1 Kings 22, 2 Chronicles 17
28. Joram	Evil	8	Obadiah	2 Kings 8–9, 11, 2 Chronicles 21
29. Ahaziah	Evil	1		2 Kings 8, 2 Chronicles 22

King	Type of King	Years Reigned	Prophets	Scripture
30. Athaliah [Queen]	Evil	6		2 Kings 11
				2 Chronicles 22–24
31. Joash	Godly	40	Joel	2 Kings 11–12
				2 Chronicles 24
32. Amaziah	Godly	29		2 Kings 15:3
				2 Chronicles 25
33. Uzziah	Godly	52		2 Kings 15
				2 Chronicles 26
34. Jotham	Godly	16	Micah	2 Kings 15
				Isaiah
				2 Chronicles 27
35. Ahaz	Evil	16	Micah	2 Kings 16
				Isaiah
				2 Chronicles 28
36. Hezekiah	Godly	29	Micah	2 Kings 18–20
				2 Chronicles 29–32
37. Manasseh	Evil	55	Nahum	2 Kings 21
				2 Chronicles 33

38.	Amon	Evil		2		2 Kings 21
						2 Chronicles 33
39.	Josiah	Godly	Zephaniah	31		2 Kings 22–23
						2 Chronicles 34–35
40.	Jehoahaz	Evil	Jeremiah	3 Months		2 Kings 23
						2 Chronicles 36
41.	Jehoiakim	Evil	Jeremiah	11		2 Kings 23–24
						Ezekiel
						2 Chronicles 36
42.	Jehoiachin	Evil	Jeremiah	3 Months		2 Kings 24
						Ezekiel
						2 Chronicles 36
43.	Zedekiah	Evil	Jeremiah	11		2 Kings 24–25
						Ezekiel
						2 Chronicles 36

LIST #22
37 Symbols and Types Found in the Bible

Symbolic language is used throughout the Bible, and theologians have developed a science of interpretation called typology. This list gives the most common types and symbols in Scripture.

1. Adam—a Type of Christ
   - Man and woman are created in God's likeness—both are called Adam.—Genesis 5:1–2
   - Adam was not deceived.—1 Timothy 2:14
   - Death enters by one man, Adam, and life enters by one man—Jesus Christ.—Romans 5:15–21

2. Amalek—a Type of the Flesh That Battles against the Spirit
   - He was the son of a concubine.—Genesis 36:12
   - Israel will war with Amalek from generation to generation.—Exodus 17:14–16
   - Amalek attacked the weakest, the weary, the feeble.—Deuteronomy 25:17–19

3. Ant—a Type of Hard Work
   - We can learn from the ant.—Proverbs 6:6
   - Ants plan ahead.—Proverbs 30:25

4. Balaam—Type of Someone Who Claims to Be a Servant of God
   - Balaam gives a blessing to Israel.
     —Numbers 22–23

- Balaam loved unrighteous wages more than he loved God.—2 Peter 2:15–16
- Balaam was in error seeking money.—Jude 1:11
- Balaam was a stumbling block.—Revelation 2:14

5. Bed—a Type with a Variety of Meanings
   - Bed of man-made programs—Isaiah 28:20
   - Bed where God's people get rest—Isaiah 57:2
   - Bed for the proud who exalt themselves —Isaiah 57:7
   - Bed of defilement—Ezekiel 23:17
   - Bed of rebellion—Hosea 7:14
   - Bed for those who are indifferent to sin —Amos 3:12
   - Bed is not a place to hide your testimony —Mark 4:21
   - Bed for those who commit adultery —Revelation 2:22

6. Brass Serpent—a Type of Christ on the Cross
   - Looking at the brass serpent saves lives. —Numbers 21:5–9
   - Jesus will be lifted up like the brass serpent. —John 3:14–15

7. Cain—a Type of the Self-Righteous Person
   - Cain offered what he thought was the right offering. —Genesis 4:1–24
   - Abel offered a more excellent sacrifice than Cain. —Hebrews 11:4
   - Cain's works were evil.—1 John 3:12
   - Cain was going the wrong way.—Jude 1:11

8. Christ—Various Types Mentioned in Scripture

- Aaron—Exodus 28:2
- Adam—Genesis 5:2
- Ark—Exodus 25:10
- Ark—[Noah's]—Genesis 6:14
- Author—Hebrews 5:9
- Body—1 Corinthians 12:12
- Branch—Zechariah 3:8
- Bread—John 6:51
- Bridegroom—Matthew 25:1
- Bull—Leviticus 1:5
- Burnt Offering—Leviticus 1:3
- Calf—Revelation 4:7
- Capstone—Psalm 118:22 (NIV)
- Captain—Hebrews 2:10
- Chief—Song of Solomon 5:10
- Commander—Isaiah 55:4
- Cornerstone—Isaiah 28:16
- David—1 Samuel 16:13
- Day—Psalm 118:24
- Donkey—Genesis 49:14
- Door—John 10:9
- Eagle—Revelation 4:7
- Flour—Leviticus 2:1
- Foundation—Isaiah 28:16
- Fountain—Zechariah 13:1
- Garment—Isaiah 61:10

- Gate—Psalm 118:20
- Gold—Isaiah 13:12
- Heir—Hebrews 1:2
- Hen—Matthew 23:37
- Hiding Place—Isaiah 32:2
- High Priest—Hebrews 4:14
- Jacob—Genesis 32:28
- Jonah—Matthew 12:40
- Joshua—Joshua 1:1
- Judge—Acts 17:31
- King—Psalm 2:6
- Lamb—Revelation 5:6
- Leaves—Revelation 22:2
- Life—John 14:6
- Light—John 8:12
- Lily of the Valley—Song of Solomon 2:1
- Lion—Revelation 5:5
- Master of House—Luke 13:25
- Meal—2 Kings 4:41 (RSV)
- Mediator—1 Timothy 2:5
- Melchizedek—Genesis 14:18
- Merchant—Matthew 13:45
- Overseer—1 Peter 2:25
- Owl—Psalm 102:6
- Ox—Ezekiel 1:10
- Passover—1 Corinthians 5:7
- Peace Offering—Leviticus 3:1

- Pelican—Psalm 102:6
- Physician—Jeremiah 8:22
- Pigeon—Leviticus 12:6
- Propitiation—Romans 3:25
- Ram—Genesis 22:13
- Resurrection—John 11:25
- Rock—Matthew 16:18
- Rock Eternal—Isaiah 26:4
- Rose of Sharon—Song of Solomon 2:1
- Root—Revelation 22:16
- Sabbath—Colossians 2:16–17
- Seed—Genesis 3:15
- Serpent—John 3:14
- Shelter—Isaiah 32:2 (NIV)
- Shepherd—John 10:11
- Sin—2 Corinthians 5:21
- Sin Offering—Leviticus 4:32
- Solomon—1 Kings 10:13
- Sower—Mark 4:3
- Sparrow—Psalm 102:7
- Star—Revelation 22:16
- Sun—Malachi 4:2
- Temple—John 2:19
- Thief—Revelation 3:3
- Tree—Revelation 22:2
- Trespass Offering—Leviticus 5:6
- Turtle Dove—Leviticus 1:14

- Truth—John 14:6
- Vine—John 15:5
- Way—John 14:6
- Worm—Psalm 22:6

9. Cross—a Type of Pain and Suffering

- To take up a cross and follow Christ is a difficult task.—Matthew 10:32–39
- The cross is foolish to some.—1 Corinthians 1:18
- The cross is offensive.—Galatians 5:11
- We have been crucified to the world. —Galatians 6:14
- Jesus despised the shame of the cross. —Hebrews 12:2

10. Death—Various Types Mentioned in Scripture

- We have died to sin.—Romans 6:2
- We were dead in sin.—Ephesians 2:1
- Death entered the world through one man. —Romans 5:12
- We died with Christ.—Romans 6:8
- We are dead to the world.—Galatians 6:14
- Our works are dead.—Hebrews 6:1; 9:14

11. Door—Various Types Mentioned in Scripture

- The Door where sin crouches—Genesis 4:7 (NIV)
- The Door of protection—Exodus 12:23
- The Door of consecration—Exodus 21:6; Deuteronomy 15:17
- The Door of heaven—Psalm 78:23

- The Door of the lazy man—Proverbs 26:14
- The Door is Christ—John 10:7–9
- The Door that is like a mouth—Micah 7:5
- The Door that shuts out distractions—Matthew 6:6
- The Door to God's answer—Luke 11:7
- The Door to the sheepfold—John 10:1
- The Door of faith—Acts 14:27
- The Door for effective work—1 Corinthians 16:9
- The Door to share Christ—Colossians 4:3
- The Door of judgment—James 5:9
- The Door to your heart—Revelation 3:20

12. Eight—a Type of Something Different

- Jesse had 8 sons; his youngest signals a new dynasty.—1 Samuel 17:12
- We can go further than expected—8 servings. —Ecclesiastes 11:2
- The 8 souls in the ark were a new beginning. —1 Peter 3:20
- A new generation starts.—Genesis 8
- The leper gets a new beginning.—Matthew 8
- There is a new revelation.—Romans 8

13. Eighteen—a Type of Deliverance and New Liberty

- Freedom is granted after 18 years of slavery. —Judges 3:12–30
- The Philistines harassed Israel for 18 years. —Judges 10:6–18
- Israel is saved from an 18-year-old despot. —2 Kings 24:6–16

- A woman is set free from an 18-year-old infirmity.
  —Luke 13:11

14. Eleven—a Type of Joining Man's Striving with Human Weakness

    - 11 stars bowing—Genesis 37:9

    - 11 sons of Israel—Genesis 42:1–5

    - 11 brothers bowing—Genesis 43:26–29

    - 11 brothers scheming for forgiveness
      —Genesis 50:15–21

    - 11 years of reign for an evil king—2 Kings 23:34–37

    - 11 disciples go to Galilee—Matthew 28:16–20

15. Example—Various Types Mentioned in Scripture

    - Abel is an example of a speaker.

    - Abraham is an example of faith.

    - Ahab is an example of ungodliness.

    - Ahijah is an example of severity.

    - Amalek is an example of the flesh.

    - Balaam is an example of greed.

    - Barnabas is an example of consolation.

    - Boaz is an example of a redeemer.

    - Caleb is an example of a man with a different spirit.

    - Daniel is an example of decisiveness.

    - David is an example of praise.

    - Delilah is an example of deception.

    - Ebedmelech is an example of kindness.

    - Elijah is an example of a reformer.

    - Elisha is an example of a helper.

- Elizabeth is an example of kindness.
- Enoch is an example of a walker.
- Esther is an example of courage.
- Gamaliel is an example of wisdom.
- Hezekiah is an example of revival.
- Isaiah is an example of spirituality.
- Jehoshaphat is an example of praise.
- Jesus is an example of every virtue.
- Jezebel is an example of bitterness.
- Job is an example of patience.
- John the Baptist is an example of devotion.
- Jonathan is an example of a friend.
- Joseph is an example of piety.
- Mordecai is an example of loyalty.
- Moses is an example of faithfulness and intercession.
- Nehemiah is an example of a godly businessman.
- Nicodemus is an example of a seeker.
- Noah is an example of a worker.
- Paul is an example of earnestness.
- Peter is an example of impulsiveness.
- Ruth is an example of humility.
- Samuel is an example of godliness and understanding.
- Saul is an example of pride.
- Timothy is an example of holiness.

16. Five—a Type of Human Weakness
    - There is an inability to live forever.—Genesis 5
    - Oppressors cannot always be avoided.—Exodus 5

- We struggle with ineptitude and poverty.
  —Leviticus 5

- Haman could not conquer Mordecai.—Esther 5

- A demon is unable to control a man.—Mark 5

- The crippled man had not been healed at the pool
  of Bethesda.—John 5

- We are unable to open the book.—Revelation 5

17. Forty—a Type of Testing

- It rained for 40 days and 40 nights.—Genesis 7:4

- The children of Israel ate manna for 40 years.
  —Exodus 16:35

- Moses spent 40 days and nights on the mountain.
  —Exodus 24:18

- Eli judged Israel for 40 years.—1 Samuel 4:18

- The children of Israel faced Goliath for 40 days.
  —1 Samuel 17:16

- David reigned as king for 40 years.—2 Samuel 5:4

- Solomon reigned as king for 40 years.
  —1 Kings 11:42

- Jesus was tested in the wilderness for 40 days.
  —Matthew 4:2

18. Four—a Type of God's Government in the Affairs
of Men

- Elijah had 4 pots of water poured on the sacrifice.
  —1 Kings 18:33

- There are 4 things that are never satisfied.
  —Proverbs 30:15

- There are 4 things in the earth too wonderful to
  understand.—Proverbs 30:18

- There are 4 things the earth cannot endure.
  —Proverbs 30:21

- There are 4 stately things upon the earth.
  —Proverbs 30:29

- The Lord will appoint 4 kinds of destruction.
  —Jeremiah 15:3

- Ezekiel saw 4 living creatures.—Ezekiel 1:5

- There are 4 winds that bring breath to the dead.
  —Ezekiel 37:9

- There were 4 men loosed and walking in the fire.
  —Daniel 3:25

- Daniel saw 4 horns in a vision.—Daniel 7:8

- There were 4 transgressions of Damascus.
  —Amos 1:3

- Zechariah saw 4 horses.—Zechariah 1:8

- The Lord showed Zechariah 4 craftsmen.
  —Zechariah 1:20

- The elect will be gathered from the 4 winds.
  —Matthew 24:31

- Lazarus was dead for 4 days.—John 11:17

- Jesus's garments were divided into 4 parts.
  —John 19:23

- There were 4 angels standing at the 4 corners of
  the earth.—Revelation 7:1

- There are 4 sides to the city of New Jerusalem.
  —Revelation 21:16

19. Hand—Various Types Mentioned in Scripture

  - The hand of authority—1 Timothy 4:14
  - The hand of concern—Proverbs 1:24

- The hand of conquering power—Exodus 14:8
- The hand of deceit—Job 31:27
- The hand of dependence—Exodus 17:12
- The hand of divine power—Exodus 6:1
- The hand of friendship—2 Kings 10:15
- The hand of human power—Genesis 9:2
- The hand of judgment—Hebrews 10:31
- The hand of remembrance—Isaiah 49:16
- The hand of restoration—2 Samuel 9:7
- The hand of salvation—Isaiah 59:1
- The hand of security—Psalm 16:8
- The hand of service—2 Kings 3:11

20. Israel—Various Types Mentioned in Scripture

- Adulterers—Hosea 7:4
- Aloes—Numbers 24:6
- Bride—Isaiah 62:5
- Brood—Luke 13:34
- Cake not turned—Hosea 7:8
- Caldron—Ezekiel 11:3
- Calves of the stall—Malachi 4:2
- Cedar trees—Numbers 24:6
- Chickens—Matthew 23:37
- Dust—Genesis 13:16
- Fig tree—Matthew 24:32
- Heifer—Hosea 4:16 (NIV)
- Jonah—Jonah 1:17
- Lion—Numbers 23:24

- Olive tree—Romans 11:17
- Sand—Genesis 22:17
- Seething pot—Jeremiah 1:13 (KJV)
- Sheep of His hand—Psalm 95:7
- Sheep of His pasture—Psalm 100:3
- Silly dove—Hosea 7:11
- Spring of water—Isaiah 58:11
- Stars—Genesis 22:17
- Trees—Psalm 104:16
- Unicorn—Numbers 24:8 (KJV)
- Vine—Ezekiel 15:6
- Virgin—2 Kings 19:21
- Watered Garden—Isaiah 58:11

21. Kiss—Various Types Mentioned in Scripture
- Kiss of affection—Song of Solomon 1:2
- Kiss of betrayal—Luke 22:48
- Kiss of connivance—Job 31:27
- Kiss of desertion—Ruth 1:14
- Kiss of devotion—Genesis 27:26
- Kiss of the enemy—Proverbs 27:6
- Kiss of farewell—Genesis 50:1
- Kiss of friendship—1 Samuel 20:41
- Kiss of gratitude—Luke 7:45
- Kiss of honor—1 Samuel 10:1
- Kiss of hypocrisy—2 Samuel 20:9
- Kiss of impudence—Proverbs 7:13
- Kiss of justice—Psalm 85:10

- Kiss of reconciliation—Genesis 45:15
- Kiss of the holy saints—Romans 16:16
- Kiss of sorrow—Acts 20:37
- Kiss of treason—2 Samuel 15:5
- Kiss of trust—Psalm 2:12

22. Law—Various Types Mentioned in Scripture
    - The Law is like a fire.—Jeremiah 23:29
    - The Law is like a lamp.—Proverbs 6:23
    - The Law is like a light.—Psalm 119:130
    - We are to delight in the Law of God. —Romans 7:22
    - We will be judged by the Law of Liberty. —James 2:12
    - The children of Israel were commanded to keep the Law of Moses.—1 Kings 2:3
    - Man cannot attain the Law of Righteousness. —Romans 9:31
    - We are to walk in the Law of the Lord. —2 Kings 10:31
    - The Law of the Spirit of life in Christ Jesus sets us free.—Romans 8:2

23. Lord—Various Types Mentioned in Scripture
    - He is Lord and Christ.—Acts 2:36
    - He is Lord of all the earth.—Joshua 3:11
    - He is Lord of all.—Acts 10:36
    - He is Lord of lords.—Deuteronomy 10:17
    - He is Lord of both the dead and the living. —Romans 14:9

- He is the Lord from heaven.—1 Corinthians 15:47
- He is the Lord of glory.—1 Corinthians 2:8
- He is the Lord of kings.—Daniel 2:47
- He is the Lord of the Sabbath.—Mark 2:28
- The Lord He is God.—Deuteronomy 4:35 (NIV)
- The Lord is a refuge.—Psalm 14:6
- The Lord surrounds His people.—Psalm 125:2
- The Lord is at hand.—Philippians 4:5
- The Lord is faithful.—2 Thessalonians 3:3
- The Lord is far from the wicked.—Proverbs 15:29
- The Lord is good.—Psalm 34:8
- The Lord is merciful and gracious.—Psalm 103:8
- The Lord is King forever.—Psalm 10:16
- The Lord is my light.—Psalm 27:1
- The Lord is my portion.—Psalm 16:5
- The Lord is my salvation.—Psalm 27:1
- The Lord is my shepherd.—Psalm 23:1
- The Lord is my shield.—Psalm 28:7
- The Lord is my strength.—Psalm 28:7
- The Lord is near to all who call upon Him.
  —Psalm 145:8
- The Lord is our shield.—Psalm 89:18
- The Lord is the Maker of all.—Proverbs 22:2
- The Lord is compassionate.—James 5:11
- The Lord is righteous.—Psalm 129:4
- The Lord is awesome.—Psalm 47:2
- The Lord is the Spirit.—2 Corinthians 3:17

- The Lord is the avenger.—1 Thessalonians 4:6
- The Lord is your keeper.—Psalm 121:5
- The Lord is your shade.—Psalm 121:5
- The Lord is upright.—Psalm 92:15

24. Manna—a Type of Christ

- Man does not live by bread alone.
  —Deuteronomy 8:3
- Christ is the living bread.—John 6:48–51
- The overcomer will eat hidden manna.
  —Revelation 2:17

25. One—a Type of Unity

- Two shall become one.—Genesis 2:24
- One law shall be for you.—Numbers 15:16
- The Lord is one.—Deuteronomy 6:4
- Christ and the Father are one.—John 10:30
- We are all one in Christ.—Galatians 3:28

26. Perfect—a Type of Maturity, Completeness,
A Different Attitude, Adequate

- Christian conversation—James 3:3–5
- Christian development—Ephesians 4:13
- Christian devotion to Christ—Matthew 19:21
- Christian discipleship—Luke 6:40
- Christian efforts and desires—Philippians 3:15
- Christians' eventual home—Hebrews 12:23
- Christians' example in Christ—Luke 13:32
- Christian experience—Hebrews 2:10
- Christians' fellowship—2 Corinthians 8:4

71

- Christian forgiveness—Matthew 5:46–48
- Christian instruction—2 Timothy 3:16
- Christians' relationship to God—John 17:23
- Christians' salvation—Colossians 1:28
- Christian training—Ephesians 6:4
- Christian understanding—1 Corinthians 2:6

27. Serpent—Various Types Mentioned in Scripture
   - A type of Satan—Genesis 3:1; Revelation 12:9
   - A type of sin—Numbers 21:6
   - A type of the Lord Jesus Christ—Numbers 21:8; 2 Corinthians 5:21; John 3:14

28. Seven—a Type of Completeness or Perfection
   - God ends His work and rests on day 7. —Genesis 2:2–3
   - Naaman the leper is cleansed after dipping himself 7 times.—2 Kings 5:10, 14
   - The number 7 signifies complete forgiveness. —Matthew 18:21–22

29. Sit—Various Types Mentioned in Scripture
   - The sitting of anticipation—Luke 9:14
   - The sitting of attentiveness—Malachi 3:3
   - The sitting of authority—Psalm 69:12
   - The sitting of determination—Psalm 1:1
   - The sitting of discouragement—2 Kings 7:3
   - The sitting of distress—Job 2:8
   - The sitting of expectation—Ruth 3:18
   - The sitting of helplessness—Isaiah 42:7

- The sitting of hopelessness—Psalm 107:10
- The sitting of humbleness—Isaiah 47:1
- The sitting of industry—Jeremiah 17:11
- The sitting of power—Psalm 29:10
- The sitting of security—Ephesians 2:6
- The sitting of sovereignty—Isaiah 40:22

30. Six—a Type of the Number of Man
    - There were to be 6 cities of refuge.—Numbers 35:6
    - There are 6 days to work.—Exodus 20:9
    - There are 2 rows of 6 loaves.—Leviticus 24:6
    - The giant had 6 fingers on each hand.
      —2 Samuel 21:20
    - The throne had 6 steps.—1 Kings 10:19
    - The number of the Antichrist is 666.
      —Revelation 13:18
    - God made man in His image on day 6.
      —Genesis 1:26–31

31. Ten—a Type of the Infirmity and Failure of Man
    - There were 10 spies.—Numbers 13:32
    - Daniel was placed on a 10-day diet.—Daniel 1:12
    - Daniel's regimen results were 10 times better than his royal counterparts.—Daniel 1:20
    - The virgins fell asleep—all 10 of them.
      —Matthew 25:1
    - Jesus healed 10 lepers.—Luke 17:12
    - A nobleman had 10 servants.—Luke 19:13

32. Thirteen—Is a Type of That Which Is Tragic and Unhappy

- The first family quarrel is recorded.—Genesis 13
- The leper is shut out of camp.—Leviticus 13
- The Jewish spies deliver an evil report.
  —Numbers 13
- The false prophet is punished.—Deuteronomy 13
- The death of Balaam is described.—Joshua 13
- Israel is delivered to the Philistines.—Judges 13
- Saul's sin is recorded.—1 Samuel 13
- Amnon rapes his sister and is murdered by his brother.—2 Samuel 13
- The death of a prophet is detailed.—1 Kings 13
- Israel is delivered into slavery.—2 Kings 13
- Uzza is killed by God.—1 Chronicles 13
- Israel is defeated by Jeroboam.—2 Chronicles 13
- David is in deep sorrow.—Psalm 13
- Hope deferred makes the heart sick.
  —Proverbs 13:12
- Babylon is destroyed.—Isaiah 13
- The destruction of Judah is foretold.—Jeremiah 13
- God condemns the prophets.—Ezekiel 13
- God pronounces judgments against Israel.
  —Hosea 13
- The wounds of Christ are foretold.—Zechariah 13
- Birds destroy the seed.—Matthew 13
- Jesus talks about the Great Tribulation.—Mark 13
- Jesus identifies Judas as the betrayer.—John 13
- Elymas is struck blind.—Acts 13
- We resist God's powers.—Romans 13

- We are as sounding brass and tinkling cymbals if we have no love.—1 Corinthians 13
- Christians are warned to avoid strange doctrines. —Hebrews 13

33. Three—a Type of Completeness
   - Faith/love/patience—1 Thessalonians 1:3
   - Word/power/Holy Spirit—1 Thessalonians 1:5
   - Turn/serve/wait—1 Thessalonians 1:9–10
   - Devoutly/justly/blamelessly—1 Thessalonians 2:10
   - Threefold salvation—2 Corinthians 1:10
   - 3 elements—Revelation 1:19
   - 3 days—Joshua 1:11
   - Resurrection on day 3—Matthew 12:40
   - 3 measures of meal—Matthew 13:33

34. Tongue—Various Types Mentioned in Scripture
   - A backbiting tongue—Proverbs 25:23
   - A burning tongue—Isaiah 30:27
   - A false tongue—Psalm 120:3
   - A fiery tongue—James 3:6
   - A lying tongue—Psalm 109:2; Proverbs 6:17
   - A tongue of many nations—Revelation 5:9
   - A perverse tongue—Proverbs 10:31
   - A prepared tongue—Psalm 45:1
   - A tongue bent as a bow—Jeremiah 9:3
   - A sharpened tongue—Psalm 140:3
   - A soft tongue—Proverbs 25:15 (KJV)
   - A stammering tongue—Isaiah 33:19

- A tongue like a sword—Psalm 64:3
- A valuable tongue—Proverbs 10:20
- A wholesome tongue—Proverbs 15:4

35. Twelve—a Type of God's Governmental Control

- There were 12 sons of Israel.—Genesis 42:13
- There were 12 stones in the breastplate of the high priest.—Exodus 28:17–20
- Jesus called 12 disciples.—Mark 3:16–19
- Moses sent 12 spies into Canaan. —Numbers 13:4–15
- Ishmael had 12 sons.—Genesis 25:13–15

36. Two—a Type of Union

- Two individuals become one.—Genesis 2:24

37. Word of God—Various Types Mentioned in Scripture

- Basin—Exodus 30:18 (NRSV)
- Bow—Habakkuk 3:9
- Buckler—Psalm 18:30 (KJV)
- Fire—Jeremiah 23:29
- Hammer—Jeremiah 23:29
- Judge—John 12:48
- Lamp—Psalm 119:105
- Light—Psalm 119:105
- Meat—1 Corinthians 3:2 (KJV)
- Milk—1 Peter 2:2
- Rain—Isaiah 55:10–11
- Seed—Luke 8:11
- Shield—Psalm 91:4

- Snow—Isaiah 55:10–11
- Spoil—Psalm 119:162 (KJV)
- Sword—Ephesians 6:17
- Truth—John 17:17
- Water—Ephesians 5:26

LIST #23
The Ministries of Elijah and Elisha

These two prophets are forever joined through their parallel ministries. Yet each ministry is distinct, as these lists will show.

The Ministry of Elijah

1. The ravens fed him.—1 Kings 17:1–6

2. He multiplied the widow's food.—1 Kings 17:8–16

3. He raised the widow's son from the dead.
   —1 Kings 17:1–24

4. He defeated the prophets of Baal.—1 Kings 18:16–46

5. He fled from Jezebel.—1 Kings 19:1–18

6. He foretold Ahab's doom.—1 Kings 21:1–29

7. He divided the Jordan River and crossed on dry ground.—2 Kings 2:1–14

8. He was taken up to heaven in a chariot.
   —2 Kings 2:1–18

The Ministry of Elisha

1. He cleansed bad water.—2 Kings 2:19–22

2. He handled taunting youths.—2 Kings 2:23–25

3. He predicted a victory.—2 Kings 3:1–25

4. He multiplied a widow's oil.—2 Kings 4:1–7

5. He promised a pregnancy. —2 Kings 4:8–17

6. He raised a dead son. —2 Kings 4:18–37

7. He purified bad food. —2 Kings 4:38–41

8. He multiplied loaves of bread. —2 Kings 4:42–44

9. He gave Gehazi leprosy. —2 Kings 5:1–27

10. He made an ax head float. —2 Kings 6:1–7

11. He trapped a Syrian army. —2 Kings 6:8–23

12. He showed the army of angels to his servant.
    —2 Kings 6:13–17

13. He predicted food for a city in famine.
    —2 Kings 6:24–7:20

▪LIST #24
10 Rewards and Crowns

Although the Christian life includes suffering and pain, this world is only temporary and heaven is eternal. This list will help you focus on and celebrate eternal rewards.

1. The judgment seat of Christ—Matthew 25:14–29; Luke 19:12–26; 1 Corinthians 3:8; Revelation 22:12

2. The reward of reigning with Christ—2 Timothy 2:12; Revelation 20:6; 22:5

3. The reward of an inheritance—Acts 20:32; Romans 8:17; Ephesians 1:14; Colossians 3:23–24

4. The reward of faithful service—Matthew 25:21; Luke 12:42–44; 2 Corinthians 4:17–18; 1 Peter 1:7

5. The reward of praise—1 Corinthians 4:5; 1 Peter 1:7

6. The imperishable crown—1 Corinthians 9:25

7. The crown of rejoicing—1 Thessalonians 2:19–20

8. The crown of righteousness—2 Timothy 4:8

9. The crown of glory—1 Peter 5:2–4

10. The crown of life—James 1:12; Revelation 2:10

■LIST #25
20 Things Missing in Heaven

Eternal life in heaven will be focused on the worship of God and the Lord Jesus. This list reveals a series of things that will *not* be in God's presence.

1. Sea—Revelation 21:1
2. Tears—Revelation 21:4
3. Death—Revelation 21:4
4. Mourning—Revelation 21:4
5. Crying—Revelation 21:4
6. Pain—Revelation 21:4
7. Sun—Revelation 21:23
8. Moon—Revelation 21:23
9. Insecurity—Revelation 21:25
10. Night—Revelation 21:25
11. Sin—Revelation 21:27
12. Sickness—Revelation 22:2
13. Lamps—Revelation 22:5
14. Devil—Revelation 20:10
15. Hunger—Revelation 7:16
16. Thirst—Revelation 7:16
17. Heat—Revelation 7:16
18. Condemnation—Romans 8:1
19. Separation—Romans 8:38–39
20. Time—I Chronicles 17:10–14

■LIST #26
8 Things Found in Heaven

As the previous list shared things that would *not* be in God's presence, here we see some things that *will*.

1. Abundance—Revelation 21:6

2. Glory—2 Corinthians 4:17

3. Rest—Revelation 14:13

4. Holiness—Revelation 21:27

5. Service—Revelation 22:3

6. Full Knowledge—1 Corinthians 13:12

7. Joy—Revelation 21:4

8. Fellowship with God—Revelation 22:3–4

LIST #27
18 Descriptions of the Kingdom of Heaven

The frequency with which the New Testament speaks of the kingdom of heaven signifies its importance.

1. A field with good and bad seed—Matthew 13:24–30
2. A small mustard seed—Matthew 13:31–32
3. Leaven—Matthew 13:33
4. A hidden treasure—Matthew 13:44
5. A businessman searching for pearls —Matthew 13:45–46
6. A large fish net—Matthew 13:47–50
7. A humble little child—Matthew 18:4
8. A king who checks up on his servants —Matthew 18:23–35
9. Hard for a rich man to get in—Matthew 19:23–26
10. A landowner who hired men to work his vineyards —Matthew 20:1–16
11. A king who prepared a banquet—Matthew 22:1–14
12. Ten wise and ten foolish virgins—Matthew 25:1–13
13. A man who entrusted property—Matthew 25:14–30
14. Soil that produces grain by itself—Mark 4:26–29
15. Within you—Luke 17:20–21
16. Not a matter of eating and drinking—Romans 14:17
17. Not a matter of talk but of power—1 Corinthians 4:20
18. Everlasting—2 Peter 1:11

LIST #28
18 Names of Satan

The many names given to Satan in the New Testament provide insight into his malevolence.

1. Abaddon—Revelation 9:11

2. Accuser—Revelation 12:10

3. Adversary—1 Peter 5:8

4. Apollyon—Revelation 9:11

5. Beelzebub—Matthew 12:24

6. Belial—2 Corinthians 6:15

7. Devil—Matthew 4:1

8. Enemy—Matthew 13:28

9. Evil One—John 17:15

10. God of This World—2 Corinthians 4:4 (KJV)

11. Liar—John 8:44

12. Murderer—John 8:44

13. Prince of the Power of the Air—Ephesians 2:2

14. Red Dragon—Revelation 12:3, 7, 9

15. Ruler of This World—John 12:31

16. Satan—Matthew 4:10

17. Serpent of Old—Revelation 12:9

18. Tempter—Matthew 4:3

■LIST #29
19 Ways the Bible Describes Hell

These 19 biblical descriptions of hell—eternal separation from God—are seriously sobering.

Hell Described as a Fire

1. Flaming fire—2 Thessalonians 1:7–8

2. This flame—Luke 16:24

3. Unquenchable fire—Matthew 3:12; Luke 3:17

4. Everlasting fire—Matthew 18:8; 25:41

5. Hell fire—Matthew 5:22; 18:9; Mark 9:47

6. Furnace of fire—Matthew 13:42, 50

7. Lake of fire—Revelation 19:20; 20:10, 14–15; 21:8

Other Descriptions of Hell

1. The worm does not die.—Mark 9:48

2. Shame and everlasting contempt—Daniel 12:2

3. A place of destruction—Matthew 7:13; Romans 9:22; Philippians 3:19

4. A place of weeping and gnashing of teeth —Matthew 13:42, 50; 22:13

5. Everlasting punishment—Matthew 25:46; Jude 1:7

6. Outer darkness—Matthew 8:12; 22:13

7. The wrath to come—Luke 3:7; Romans 5:9; 1 Thessalonians 1:10

8. A place of torment—Luke 16:28; Revelation 14:11; 20:10

9. Everlasting destruction—2 Thessalonians 1:9

10. A place of damnation or condemnation—Jude 1:4

11. A place of retribution—2 Corinthians 11:15; 2 Thessalonians 1:6; Revelation 20:13

12. The second death—Revelation 20:14; 21:8

LIST #30
14 Important Mountains in the Bible

The mountains in this list have played significant roles in biblical history.

1. Mount Ararat—Where Noah landed the Ark —Genesis 8:4

2. Mount Carmel—Where Elijah fought with the prophets of Baal—1 Kings 18:9–42

3. Mount Ebal—Where Moses built an altar —Deuteronomy 27:4

4. Mount Gerizim—Where Jesus met the woman at the well—John 4:20

5. Mount Gilboa—Where King Saul was killed —1 Chronicles 10:1, 8

6. Mount Hermon—Where a boundary line was established—Joshua 11:3, 17

7. Mount Lebanon—Where Solomon got his cedar wood—1 Kings 5:14

8. Mount Moriah—Where Abraham took Isaac to sacrifice—Genesis 22:2

9. Mount Nebo—Where Moses looked at the Promised Land—Deuteronomy 34:1

10. Mount Olivet—Where Jesus spoke of His second coming—Matthew 24:3

11. Mount Seir—Where Esau Lived—Genesis 36:8

12. Mount Sinai—Where Moses received the Law of God
    —Exodus 19:2–25

13. Mount Tabor—Where Barak attacked Sisera
    —Judges 4:6–15

14. Mount Zion—The site of Jerusalem
    —Lamentations 1:4; 2 Samuel 5:7

LIST #31
15 Types of Faith

These descriptions of faith serve to inspire us to grow in our own.

1. Great faith—Matthew 8:10

2. Mustard seed faith—Matthew 17:20

3. Strong faith—Romans 4:20

4. Weak faith—Romans 14:1

5. Steadfast faith—Colossians 2:5

6. Sincere faith—1 Timothy 1:5

7. Shipwrecked faith—1 Timothy 1:19–20

8. Bold faith—1 Timothy 3:13

9. First faith—1 Timothy 5:12

10. Overthrown faith—2 Timothy 2:18

11. Common faith—Titus 1:4

12. Sound faith—Titus 1:13

13. Rich faith—James 2:5

14. Precious faith—2 Peter 1:1

15. No faith—Mark 4:40

LIST #32
40 Things That Happen at Conversion

In an instant, the life of a person is transformed through a personal relationship with Jesus Christ. This list highlights this changed life.

1. Adoption—Romans 8:14–23
2. Redemption—Romans 3:24–25
3. Propitiation—Romans 3:24–25; 4:7
4. Imputation—Romans 4:1–11
5. Reconciliation—Romans 5:10
6. Substitution—Romans 4:3–25
7. Sonship—John 1:12
8. Heir—Romans 8:17
9. Righteousness—Romans 3:21–4:25
10. Ransom—Matthew 20:28
11. Remission—Matthew 26:28
12. Sanctification—1 Corinthians 6:11
13. Justification—1 Corinthians 6:11
14. Washing—1 Corinthians 6:11
15. Preservation—John 10:27–29
16. Acceptance with God—Ephesians 1:6
17. Perfection—Hebrews 10:14

18. Made fit—Colossians 1:12

19. Translated—Colossians 1:13

20. Made rich—Ephesians 1:3

21. Predestined—Romans 8:29–30

22. Chosen—Ephesians 1:4

23. Regeneration—Titus 3:5

24. Forgiveness—Ephesians 1:7

25. Deliverance from Satan—Colossians 1:13

26. Deliverance from self—Romans 6:6

27. Deliverance from the law—Romans 6:14

28. Faith—Romans 12:3

29. Called—Acts 2:38–39

30. Access to God—Romans 5:2

31. Assurance—1 John 5:13

32. Wisdom—1 Corinthians 1:30

33. Holy Spirit—John 14:16–17

34. Fruit of the Spirit—Galatians 5:22–23

35. Gifts of the Spirit—1 Corinthians 7:7; 12:7, 11

36. Eternal life—1 John 5:11–12

37. Called Christian—Acts 11:26

38. Made salt—Matthew 5:13

39. Made servants—1 Corinthians 7:22

40. Made an ambassador—2 Corinthians 5:20

LIST #33
15 Keys to Wisdom

Wisdom is knowledge prudently applied.

1. Wisdom makes a man happy.—Proverbs 3:13

2. Wisdom is more precious than rubies.
   —Proverbs 3:15

3. Wisdom is the principal thing.—Proverbs 4:7

4. Seek wisdom early.—Proverbs 8:17 (KJV)

5. There are treasures in wisdom.—Proverbs 8:21

6. To fear the Lord is the beginning of wisdom.
   —Proverbs 9:10

7. Wisdom is pure.—James 3:17

8. Wisdom is peaceable.—James 3:17

9. Wisdom is gentle.—James 3:17

10. Wisdom is willing to yield.—James 3:17

11. Wisdom is full of mercy.—James 3:17

12. Wisdom is full of good fruits.—James 3:17

13. Wisdom does not show partiality.—James 3:17

14. Wisdom is not filled with hypocrisy.—James 3:17

15. If you want wisdom, ask God for it.—James 1:5

■LIST #34
28 Things the Bible Says about Sex

The Bible speaks candidly about sex in these 28 references.

1. Do not commit adultery.—Exodus 20:14

2. Do not covet another man's wife.—Exodus 20:17

3. Do not have sex with your father.—Leviticus 18:7

4. Do not have sex with your mother.—Leviticus 18:7

5. Do not have sex with your stepmother.
   —Leviticus 18:8

6. Do not have sex with your sister or stepsister.
   —Leviticus 18:9

7. Do not have sex with your granddaughter.
   —Leviticus 18:10

8. Do not have sex with your aunts.—Leviticus 8:12–13

9. Do not have sex with your uncles.—Leviticus 18:14

10. Do not have sex with your daughter-in-law.
    —Leviticus 18:15

11. Do not have sex with your sister-in-law.
    —Leviticus 18:16

12. Do not have sex with a woman and her daughter.
    —Leviticus 18:17

13. Do not have sex with a woman and her granddaughter.
    —Leviticus 18:17

14. Do not have sex with two sisters.—Leviticus 18:18

15. Do not have sex with a person of the same sex.
    —Leviticus 18:22

16. Do not have sex with an animal.—Leviticus 18:23

17. Do not make your daughter into a prostitute.
    —Leviticus 19:29

18. Do not be involved in cross-dressing.
    —Deuteronomy 22:5

19. Do not get someone drunk so you can see their
    nakedness.—Habakkuk 2:15

20. Do not lust after a woman in your heart.
    —Matthew 5:28

21. Do not be involved with sexual immorality.
    —Acts 15:29

22. Do not be involved with homosexual acts.
    —Romans 1:26–28

23. Sexual immorality is a sin against your own body.
    —1 Corinthians 6:18

24. Avoid sexual immorality—get married.
    —1 Corinthians 7:2

25. Husbands and wives should not deprive each other
    of sex.—1 Corinthians 7:4–5

26. God's will is for mankind to abstain from sexual
    immorality.—1 Thessalonians 4:3–8

27. The marriage bed is blessed by God.—Hebrews 13:4

28. Eyes filled with lust come from the world, not God.
    —1 John 2:16

LIST #35
10 Long and Short Things in the Bible

Just for fun, explore this list of "longests" and "shortests."

1. Longest book in the Old Testament—Psalms with 150 chapters and 2,461 verses

2. Shortest book in the Old Testament—Obadiah with 21 verses and 670 words

3. Longest book in the New Testament—Luke with 24 chapters and 1,151 verses

4. Shortest book in the New Testament—2 John with 13 verses and 298 words

5. Longest chapter in the Bible—Psalm 119 with 176 verses

6. Shortest chapter in the Bible—Psalm 117 with 2 verses

7. Longest verse in the Bible—Esther 8:9 with 90 words

8. Shortest verse in the Bible—John 11:35 with 2 words

9. Longest prayer in the Bible—Nehemiah 9:5–38

10. Shortest prayer in the Bible—Matthew 14:30 with 3 words

LIST #36
18 of the Oldest People in the Bible

In the period of history before the Flood, people lived much longer than we do today. Here are the names and ages of those with the greatest longevity.

1. Methuselah lived for 969 years.—Genesis 5:27
2. Jared lived for 962 years.—Genesis 5:20
3. Noah lived 950 years.—Genesis 9:29
4. Adam lived 930 years.—Genesis 5:5
5. Seth lived 912 years.—Genesis 5:8
6. Kenan lived 910 years.—Genesis 5:14
7. Enos lived 905 years.—Genesis 5:11
8. Mahalaleel lived 895 years.—Genesis 5:17
9. Lamech lived 777 years.—Genesis 5:31
10. Shem lived 600 years.—Genesis 11:10–11
11. Eber lived 464 years.—Genesis 11:16–17
12. Arphaxad lived 438 years.—Genesis 11:12–13
13. Salah lived 433 years.—Genesis 11:14–15
14. Enoch lived 365 years.—Genesis 5:23
15. Peleg lived 239 years.—Genesis 11:18–19
16. Reu lived 239 years.—Genesis 11:20–21
17. Serug lived 230 years.—Genesis 11:22–23
18. Nahor lived 148 years.—Genesis 11:24–25

LIST #37
17 Lost, Hidden, and Mysterious Books

These Old Testament references allude to books that have mysteriously disappeared or were lost and never recovered.

1. Book of the Wars of the Lord—Numbers 21:14–15

2. Book of Jasher—Joshua 10:13

3. A secret book that came to Joshua—Joshua 18:9

4. Samuel's book about the behavior of royalty —1 Samuel 10:25

5. The Acts of Solomon—1 Kings 11:41

6. Book of the Kings of Israel—1 Chronicles 9:1

7. Samuel the Seer—1 Chronicles 29:29

8. Nathan the Prophet—1 Chronicles 29:29; 2 Chronicles 9:29

9. Gad the Seer—1 Chronicles 29:29

10. Prophecy of Ahijah the Shilonite—2 Chronicles 9:29

11. Shemaiah the Prophet—2 Chronicles 12:15

12. Iddo the Seer—2 Chronicles 9:29; 12:15

13. Jehu the Son of Hanani—2 Chronicles 20:34

14. The Records of the Fathers—Ezra 4:15

15. The Book of the Chronicles—Esther 2:21–23

16. The Unknown Book—record of Purim—Esther 9:32

17. The Chronicles of the Kings of Media and Persia —Esther 10:2

LIST #38
25 Animals in God's Special Zoo

Many animals appear in the Bible, but these 25 animals played a special role in the stories of Scripture.

1. Abraham sacrificed a ram instead of Isaac.
   —Genesis 22:13

2. The rod of Moses was turned into a serpent.
   —Exodus 4:3

3. Frogs were one of the ten plagues on the Egyptians.
   —Exodus 8:6

4. Lice were one of the ten plagues on the Egyptians.
   —Exodus 8:17

5. The Egyptians were swatting the flies.—Exodus 8:22

6. Close your mouth, the locusts are coming.
   —Exodus 10:13

7. Anyone for a little quail for dinner?—Exodus 16:13

8. Don't step on the fiery serpents.—Numbers 21:6

9. Balaam heard from a talking donkey.—Numbers 22:28

10. Two cows pulled the cart to transport the ark.
    —1 Samuel 6:7–12

11. A lion waited for the disobedient prophet.
    —1 Kings 13:24, 28

12. Ravens brought food for the prophet Elijah.
    —1 Kings 17:6

13. Horses of fire pulled a chariot of heaven.
    —2 Kings 2:11

14. Two wild she bears mauled the taunting youths.
    —2 Kings 2:24

15. The dogs had Jezebel for dinner.—2 Kings 9:36

16. God caused the lions to have "lockjaw."—Daniel 6:22

17. God caused a big fish to swallow Jonah.—Jonah 1:17

18. A worm devoured Jonah's shade plant.—Jonah 4:7

19. Peter found money in a fish.—Matthew 17:27

20. Jesus rode the colt of a donkey into Jerusalem.
    —Zechariah 9:9; Matthew 21:7

21. A crowing rooster reminded Peter of Jesus's words.
    —Matthew 26:74–75

22. Jesus sent demons into the pigs (deviled ham!).
    —Mark 5:13

23. Jesus multiplied the fish to feed thousands.
    —Mark 8:6–9; John 6:9–12

24. Jesus provided a great catch of fish.—Luke 5:5–6;
    John 21:2–6

25. Paul was unharmed by a venomous viper.
    —Acts 28:3–6

LIST #39
10 Giants like Goliath

The most famous giant in the Bible is Goliath (1 Samuel 17:4). But here are 10 other passages where giants also appear.

1. There were giants in the land before Noah and the Flood.—Genesis 6:4

2. The giants called Rephaim existed at the time of Abraham.—Genesis 15:18–20

3. The sons of Anak were giants.—Numbers 13:33

4. There were giants known as Emims.
   —Deuteronomy 2:9–11

5. The Zamzummims were giants.
   —Deuteronomy 2:19–21

6. The giant named Og of Bashan had a large bed.
   —Deuteronomy 3:11

7. There was a giant named Arba.—Joshua 14:15

8. Anak was a giant.—Joshua 15:13

9. Sheshai, Ahiman, and Talmai were giants.
   —Joshua 15:14

10. The brothers of Goliath were—Saph, Lahmi, and Ishbi-benob. One of the brothers had six fingers on each hand and six toes on each foot.—2 Samuel 1:16–22; 1 Chronicles 20:4–8

LIST #40
21 Angels in the Bible

The Bible records at least 21 references to angels appearing to man.

1. An angel appeared to Hagar.—Genesis 16:1–12

2. Two angels rescued Lot.—Genesis 19:1–22

3. An angel spoke to Abraham.—Genesis 22:1–18

4. An angel wrestled with Jacob.—Genesis 32:24–30

5. An angel appeared to Moses.—Exodus 3:2–4:17

6. An angel dealt with Balaam.—Numbers 22:22–35

7. An angel confronted Joshua before battle.
    —Joshua 5:13–15

8. An angel appeared to Gideon.—Judges 6:11–23

9. An angel spoke to Samson's parents.
    —Judges 13:1–20

10. An angel dealt with Elijah.—1 Kings 19:1–8

11. There was an angel at Jesus's tomb.
    —Matthew 28:5–7; Mark 16:5–7

12. The angel Gabriel appeared to Zacharias.
    —Luke 1:5–22

13. The angel Gabriel appeared to Mary.—Luke 1:26–38

14. An angel appeared to Joseph.
    —Matthew 1:20–21

15. An angel announced the birth of Jesus.
    —Luke 2:8–15

16. Angels spoke to the disciples at the ascension.
    —Acts 1:9–11

17. An angel released the apostles.—Acts 5:17–20

18. An angel told Philip to go to Gaza.—Acts 8:26–39

19. An angel appeared to Cornelius.—Acts 10:1–8

20. An angel helped Peter escape from prison.
    —Acts 12:1–19

21. An angel spoke to Paul.—Acts 27:21–25

LIST #41
30 "Be" Commands in the Bible

Many New Testament commandments were spoken in simple "Be" statements. These directives are to be taken seriously.

1. Be glad.—Matthew 5:12

2. Be reconciled to your brother.—Matthew 5:24

3. Be witnesses.—Acts 1:8

4. Be baptized.—Acts 2:38

5. Be devoted to one another.—Romans 12:10

6. Be joyful, hopeful, patient, faithful.—Romans 12:12

7. Be willing to associate.—Romans 12:16

8. Be careful to do right.—Romans 12:17

9. Be reconciled to God.—2 Corinthians 5:20

10. Be separate.—2 Corinthians 6:17

11. Be of one mind.—2 Corinthians 13:11

12. Be humble and gentle.—Ephesians 4:2

13. Be kind and compassionate.—Ephesians 4:32

14. Be imitators of God.—Ephesians 5:1

15. Be careful how you live.—Ephesians 5:15

16. Be filled with the Spirit.—Ephesians 5:18

17. Be strong in the Lord.—Ephesians 6:10

18. Be alert.—Ephesians 6:18

19. Be thankful.—Colossians 3:15

20. Be wise to unbelievers.—Colossians 4:5

21. Be patient.—1 Thessalonians 5:14

22. Be joyful always.—1 Thessalonians 5:16

23. Be content.—Hebrews 13:5

24. Be quick to listen, slow to speak, slow to be angry.
—James 1:19

25. Be holy.—1 Peter 1:16

26. Be sympathetic, compassionate, humble.
—1 Peter 3:8 (RSV)

27. Be prepared to give an answer.—1 Peter 3:15

28. Be clear minded and self-controlled.—1 Peter 4:7

29. Be eager to make your calling and election sure.
—2 Peter 1:10

30. Be merciful.—Jude 1:22 (RSV)

■LIST #42
25 Promises from the Psalms

These beautiful promises can be used for your personal praise and worship.

1. You shall prosper.—Psalm 1:1–3
2. You shall have hope.—Psalm 16:8–9
3. You shall have joy.—Psalm 16:11
4. You shall be delivered.—Psalm 18:19
5. You will be rewarded.—Psalm 18:20
6. You will receive mercy.—Psalm 18:25
7. You will be restored.—Psalm 23:3
8. You will fear no evil.—Psalm 23:4
9. You will be strengthened.—Psalm 27:14
10. You will be blessed.—Psalm 32:1
11. You will not fear.—Psalm 34:4
12. You will be provided for.—Psalm 34:9–10
13. You will overcome trouble.—Psalm 34:17
14. You will have your heart's desires.—Psalm 37:4
15. You will have peace.—Psalm 37:11
16. You will be led.—Psalm 37:23–24
17. You will have strength in troubled times.—Psalm 37:39

18. You will have the Lord's ear.—Psalm 40:1

19. You will have answers to prayer.—Psalm 55:17

20. You need not be afraid.—Psalm 56:11

21. You will receive power.—Psalm 68:35

22. You will not be afraid of night.—Psalm 91:5

23. You will not stumble.—Psalm 119:165

24. You will be preserved from evil.—Psalm 121:5–6

25. You will draw close to God.—Psalm 145:18

LIST #43
Memorizing Old Testament Books Made Simple

Use this poem to help you recall the simple truths in each Old Testament book.

In Genesis the world began;
'Twas then that God created man.

In Exodus the law was given,
As Israel's guide from earth to heaven.

Leviticus, from Levi's name,
The tribe from which the priesthood came.

Then Numbers tells about the way
What God would have us do and say.

Deuteronomy, which means "twice told,"
The truth, once heard, must ne'er grow old.

Then Joshua came, in Moses' place,
When law had failed, God brought in grace.

He next by Judges Israel ruled;
His love toward them never cooled.

And then, the story sweet of Ruth,
Foreshadows very precious truth.

In Samuel First we read of Saul
The people's king—his rise and fall.

In Second Samuel then we hear
Of David—man of God so dear.

In First of Kings the glory filled
The Temple Solomon did build.

And Second Kings records the lives
Of prophets, kings, their sons, and wives.

In First of Chronicles we're shown
The house of David and his throne.

And Second Chronicles records
King Solomon's good deeds and words.

Then Ezra builds God's house again,
Which had for long in ruins lain.

And Nehemiah builds the wall
Round Judah's city, great and tall.

Then Esther, Jewish maid and wife,
Raised up to save her people's life.

And Job his patience sorely tried
At last God's dealings justified.

Then comes the Psalms, whose sacred page
Is full of truth for every age.

The Proverbs, which the wise man spake,
For all who will their teaching take.

Ecclesiastes shows how vain
The very best of earthly gain.

The Song, how much we need to prize
The treasures set above the skies.

Isaiah, first of prophets, who
Foretells the future of the Jew.

Then Jeremiah scorned by foes,
Yet weeps for faithless Israel's woes.

The Lamentations tell in part
The sadness of this prophet's heart.

Ezekiel tells us, in mystic story,
Departing and returning glory.

Then Daniel, from the lions' den,
By power Divine is raised again.

Hosea shows the Father's heart
So grieved for sin on Ephraim's part.

And Joel tells of judgment near;
The wicked nations quake and fear.

Then Amos from the herdmen sent,
Calls hardened sinners to repent.

In Obadiah, Edom's fall
Contains a warning word to all.

Jonah, though prophet of the Lord,
Yet fled to Tarshish from his word.

Then Micah sings in sweetest lays
The glory of millennial days.

And Nahum tells the fear and gloom
Of Nineveh and her doom.

Habakkuk—though the fig-tree fail,
His faith and trust in God prevail.

Then Zephaniah tells of grace,
And love that comes in judgment's place.

And Haggai in the latter days,
Repeats: consider well your ways.

In Zechariah's wondrous book,
We find eight visions if we look.

Then Malachi, the last of all,
Speaks sadly still of Israel's fall.

—E. J. Carr, London, 1890

LIST #44
240 One-Time Words in the Bible

2,300 words are mentioned only once in the Bible. Here's a list of 240 of the most notable examples from the King James Version of the Bible.

1. Afternoon—Judges 19:8

2. Anna—Luke 2:36

3. Ancestors—Leviticus 26:45

4. Anvil—Isaiah 41:7

5. Aunt—Leviticus 18:14

6. Backbiters—Romans 1:30

7. Backslider—Proverbs 14:14

8. Backbone—Leviticus 3:9

9. Ball—Isaiah 22:18

10. Barber's—Ezekiel 5:1

11. Beacon—Isaiah 30:17

12. Benches—Ezekiel 27:6

13. Benefactors—Luke 22:25

14. Betrayers—Acts 7:52

15. Blaze—Mark 1:45

16. Bosses—Job 15:26

17. Bowmen—Jeremiah 4:29

18. Bribery—Job 15:34

19. Cab—2 Kings 6:25

20. Cabins—Jeremiah 37:16

21. Candles—Zephaniah 1:12

22. Castor—Acts 28:11

23. Chapel—Amos 7:13

24. Charmed—Jeremiah 8:17

25. Chatter—Isaiah 38:14

26. Checker work—1 Kings 7:17

27. Cheekbone—Psalm 3:7

28. Chickens—Matthew 23:37

29. Chimney—Hosea 13:3

30. Coffin—Genesis 50:26

31. Colony—Acts 16:12

32. Confectionaries—1 Samuel 8:13

33. Conquerors—Romans 8:37

34. Constellations—Isaiah 13:10

35. Coppersmith—2 Timothy 4:14

36. Cousin—Luke 1:36

37. Cracknels—1 Kings 14:3

38. Creditors—Isaiah 50:1

39. Cripple—Acts 14:8

40. Crisping pins—Isaiah 3:22

41. Cupbearer—Nehemiah 1:11

42. Damnable—2 Peter 2:1

43. Dealer—Isaiah 21:2

44. Decently—1 Corinthians 14:40

45. Defamed—1 Corinthians 4:13

46. Delicacies—Revelation 18:3

47. Detest—Deuteronomy 7:26

48. Devilish—James 3:15

49. Discerner—Hebrews 4:12

50. Disgrace—Jeremiah 14:21

51. Doctor—Acts 5:34

52. Drinks—Hebrews 9:10

53. Dropsy—Luke 14:2

54. Dryshod—Isaiah 11:15

55. Dues—Romans 13:7

56. Dwarf—Leviticus 21:20

57. Easter—Acts 12:4

58. Empire—Esther 1:20

59. Evangelists—Ephesians 4:11

60. Evenings—Jeremiah 5:6

61. Execution—Esther 9:1

62. Eyebrows—Leviticus 14:9

63. Farm—Matthew 22:5

64. Fashions—Ezekiel 42:11

65. Ferry—2 Samuel 19:18

66. Fishhooks—Amos 4:2

67. Flag—Job 8:11

68. Forgers—Job 13:4

69. Freckled—Leviticus 13:39

70. Frozen—Job 38:30

71. Gardener—John 20:15

72. Gay—James 2:3

73. Grandmother—2 Timothy 1:5

74. Grease—Psalm 119:70

75. Greyhound—Proverbs 30:31

76. Gulf—Luke 16:26

77. Handkerchiefs—Acts 19:12

78. Hats—Daniel 3:21

79. Heresy—Acts 24:14

80. Immortal—1 Timothy 1:17

81. Influences—Job 38:31

82. Intelligence—Daniel 11:30

83. Inventors—Romans 1:30

84. Itch—Deuteronomy 28:27

85. Juice—Song of Songs 8:2

86. Julia—Romans 16:15

87. Kettle—1 Samuel 2:14

88. Kicked—Deuteronomy 32:15

89. Ladder—Genesis 28:12

90. Landmarks—Job 24:2

91. Lanterns—John 18:3

92. Lioness—Ezekiel 19:2

93. Liquors—Exodus 22:29

94. Looking glass—Job 37:18

95. Lukewarm—Revelation 3:16

96. Magician—Daniel 2:10

97. Magnificence—Acts 19:27

98. Malefactor—John 18:30

99. Malicious—3 John 1:10

100. Mansions—John 14:2

101. Martyrs—Revelation 17:6

102. Masterbuilder—1 Corinthians 3:10

103. Mealtime—Ruth 2:14

104. Meddled—Proverbs 17:14

105. Melons—Numbers 11:5

106. Mile—Matthew 5:41

107. Millions—Genesis 24:60

108. Minstrel—2 Kings 3:15

109. Modest—1 Timothy 2:9

110. Moles—Isaiah 2:20

111. Monuments—Isaiah 65:4

112. Mortgaged—Nehemiah 5:3

113. Mourner—2 Samuel 14:2

114. Mufflers—Isaiah 3:19

115. Muse—Psalm 143:5

116. Musicians—Revelation 18:22

117. Nailing—Colossians 2:14

118. Necromancer—Deuteronomy 18:11

119. News—Proverbs 25:25

120. Novice—1 Timothy 3:6

121. Oar—Ezekiel 27:29

122. Observer—Deuteronomy 18:10

123. Onions—Numbers 11:5

124. Opinions—1 Kings 18:21

125. Oration—Acts 12:21

126. Orchard—Song of Songs 4:13

127. Orphans—Lamentations 5:3

128. Ostrich—Job 39:13

129. Outcast—Jeremiah 30:17

130. Outlandish—Nehemiah 13:26

131. Outrageous—Proverbs 27:4

132. Ovens—Exodus 8:3

133. Overcharged—Luke 21:34

134. Overspread—Genesis 9:19

135. Overwhelm—Job 6:27

136. Owe—Romans 13:8

137. Paddle—Deuteronomy 23:13

138. Painting—Jeremiah 4:30

139. Parlours—1 Chronicles 28:11

140. Parties—Exodus 22:9

141. Pastor—Jeremiah 17:16

142. Patterns—Hebrews 9:23

143. Paws—Leviticus 11:27

144. Payment—Matthew 18:25

145. Pedigrees—Numbers 1:18

146. Penknife—Jeremiah 36:23

147. Philosophers—Acts 17:18

148. Phylacteries—Matthew 23:5

149. Pipers—Revelation 18:22

150. Planets—2 Kings 23:5

151. Plantation—Ezekiel 17:7

152. Policy—Daniel 8:25

153. Polishing—Lamentations 4:7

154. Portray—Ezekiel 4:1

155. Presbytery—1 Timothy 4:14

156. Prices—Acts 4:34

157. Princess—Lamentations 1:1

158. Private—2 Peter 1:20

159. Prognosticators—Isaiah 47:13

160. Providence—Acts 24:2

161. Psalmist—2 Samuel 23:1

162. Pulpit—Nehemiah 8:4

163. Quantity—Isaiah 22:24

164. Quicksands—Acts 27:17

165. Quivered—Habakkuk 3:16

166. Ragged—Isaiah 2:21

167. Reaper—Amos 9:13

168. Rebuker—Hosea 5:2

169. Recorded—Nehemiah 12:22

170. Reformation—Hebrews 9:10

171. Remembrances—Job 13:12

172. Revengers—2 Samuel 14:11

173. Reverend—Psalm 111:9

174. Rewarder—Hebrews 11:6

175. Rifled—Zechariah 14:2

176. Ringleader—Acts 24:5

177. Rip—2 Kings 8:12

178. Rites—Numbers 9:3

179. Rovers—1 Chronicles 12:21

180. Rubbing—Luke 6:1

181. Rude—2 Corinthians 11:6

182. Sacrilege—Romans 2:22

183. Sadness—Ecclesiastes 7:3

184. Sailors—Revelation 18:17

185. Sap—Psalm 104:16

186. Scaffold—2 Chronicles 6:13

187. Scalp—Psalm 68:21

188. Scorch—Revelation 16:8

189. Seedtime—Genesis 8:22

190. Senators—Psalm 105:22

191. Shearer—Acts 8:32

192. Sheepskins—Hebrews 11:37

193. Shoulder blade—Job 31:22

194. Shroud—Ezekiel 31:3

195. Screech owl—Isaiah 34:14

196. Sighs—Lamentations 1:22

197. Sister in law—Ruth 1:15

198. Slave—Jeremiah 2:14

199. Snorting—Jeremiah 8:16

200. Snout—Proverbs 11:22

201. Spectacle—1 Corinthians 4:9

202. Spiced—Song of Songs 8:2

203. Spite—Psalm 10:14

204. Spitting—Isaiah 50:6

205. Spokesman—Exodus 4:16

206. Sprout—Job 14:7

207. Stacks—Exodus 22:6

208. Stamping—Jeremiah 47:3

209. Stargazers—Isaiah 47:13

210. Stoicks—Acts 17:18

211. Stomach's—1 Timothy 5:23

212. Stripling—1 Samuel 17:56

213. Sue—Matthew 5:40

214. Sundry—Hebrews 1:1

215. Supped—1 Corinthians 11:25

216. Supreme—1 Peter 2:13

217. Tattlers—1 Timothy 5:13

218. Taverns—Acts 28:15

219. Taxes—Daniel 11:20

220. Temper—Ezekiel 46:14

221. Traitor—Luke 6:16

222. Treachery—2 Kings 9:23

223. Tutors—Galatians 4:2

224. Usurp—1 Timothy 2:12

225. Vagabonds—Psalm 109:10

226. Vomited—Jonah 2:10

227. Voyage—Acts 27:10

228. Wagon—Numbers 7:3

229. Waterspouts—Psalm 42:7

230. Weasel—Leviticus 11:29

231. Wedlock—Ezekiel 16:38

232. Western—Numbers 34:6

233. Wines—Isaiah 25:6

234. Wintered—Acts 28:11

235. Wires—Exodus 39:3

236. Wit's—Palm 107:27

237. Worker—1 Kings 7:14

238. Wreath—2 Chronicles 4:13

239. Yoked—2 Corinthians 6:14

240. Youthful—2 Timothy 2:22

LIST #45
96 Godly Character Traits

Adopting these godly character traits will help every Christian grow to be more Christlike.

1. Abstinence from all appearances of evil
   —1 Thessalonians 5:22

2. Attentiveness—Proverbs 22:17

3. Attentiveness to Christ's voice—John 10:3–4

4. Availability—Matthew 16:25

5. Belief in Christ—John 6:29; 1 John 3:23

6. Blamelessness and harmlessness—Philippians 2:15

7. Boldness—Proverbs 28:1; Romans 13:3;
   Ephesians 6:19–20

8. Cautiousness—James 1:19; Proverbs 21:5

9. Compassion—1 John 3:17

10. Contentment—Philippians 4:11; Hebrews 13:5

11. Contriteness—Isaiah 57:15; 66:2; Psalms 34:18;
    51:17

12. Control of the body—1 Corinthians 9:27;
    Colossians 3:5

13. Creativity—Proverbs 8:12; James 1:5

14. Decisiveness—Philippians 3:14; James 1:8

15. Deference—Hebrews 12:3

16. Dependability—Luke 16:10; Revelation 2:10; Philippians 4:13

17. Determination—Proverbs 28:1

18. Devotion—Acts 8:2; 22:12

19. Diligence—Proverbs 10:4; 22:29

20. Discernment—Ezekiel 44:23; Hebrews 5:14

21. Discretion—Proverbs 17:28; 27:12; James 1:19

22. Doing the Lord's work—1 Corinthians 15:58

23. Endurance—2 Timothy 2:3; Hebrews 12:1

24. Enthusiasm—Romans 12:9–11; Galatians 4:18

25. Faithfulness—Revelation 17:14

26. Faith—2 Corinthians 5:7; James 2:17–18

27. Fear of God—Acts 10:2

28. Flexibility—1 Corinthians 9:22

29. Following after good—Philippians 4:8; 1 Thessalonians 5:15

30. Following Christ—John 10:4, 27

31. Forgiveness—Psalm 130:4; Matthew 6:14; 18:21–22; Proverbs 19:11

32. Generosity—2 Corinthians 9:6; Luke 6:38

33. Gentleness—James 3:17; Titus 3:2

34. God-taught—Isaiah 54:13; 1 John 2:27

35. Godliness—Psalm 4:3; 2 Peter 2:9

36. Gratefulness—Psalm 116:17; Hebrews 13:15

37. Guileless—John 1:47

38. Hatred of defilement—Jude 1:23

39. Holiness—Deuteronomy 7:6; 14:2; Colossians 3:12

40. Honesty—1 Thessalonians 4:12

41. Honor—1 Thessalonians 5:12–13; Romans 13:3–4

42. Honor toward others—Psalm 15:4; Romans 12:10

43. Hospitality—1 Peter 4:9; James 2:15–16

44. Humility—Psalm 34:2; 1 Peter 5:5

45. Hunger after righteousness—Matthew 5:6

46. Initiative—Galatians 6:10

47. Joyfulness—Psalm 16:11; Nehemiah 8:10

48. Just—Genesis 6:9; Habakkuk 2:4; Luke 2:25

49. Justice—Proverbs 4:18; 24:18; Micah 6:8

50. Liberality—Acts 20:35; Romans 12:13

51. Love—Colossians 1:4; 1 Thessalonians 4:9

52. Lowliness—Proverbs 16:19

53. Loyalty—John 6:66–68

54. Meekness—Matthew 11:29; 1 Peter 3:3–4;
Isaiah 29:19; Matthew 5:5

55. Mercy—Psalm 37:26; Matthew 5:7

56. New Creature—2 Corinthians 5:17; Ephesians 2:10

57. Obedience—John 10:27; 14:15; Romans 16:19;
1 Peter 1:14; 1 John 5:3

58. Orderliness—1 Corinthians 14:33, 40

59. Overcoming the world—1 John 5:4–5

60. Patience—Romans 5:3–4; 2 Timothy 2:24

61. Peaceful—Romans 12:18; Hebrews 12:14

62. Persuasiveness—2 Corinthians 4:2

63. Poor in Spirit—Psalm 51:17; Matthew 5:3

64. Prudence—Proverbs 16:21

65. Punctuality—Ephesians 5:15–16

66. Purity of heart—Matthew 5:8; 1 John 3:3

67. Putting away sin—1 Corinthians 5:7; Hebrews 12:1

68. Rejoicing in Christ—Philippians 3:1; 4:4

69. Rejoicing in God—Psalm 33:1; Habakkuk 3:18

70. Resourcefulness—Matthew 7:7–8; 25:15–27

71. Responsibility—Ephesians 6:1–8; 1 Peter 3:1–7;
Proverbs 25:19; 1 Corinthians 4:2; Colossians 3:23–24

72. Righteousness—Isaiah 60:21; Luke 1:6

73. Security—Isaiah 30:15; Psalm 27:1–3

74. Self-Control—Romans 12:2; 1 Corinthians 9:24–25

75. Sensitivity—Romans 12:15; 1 Peter 3:8

76. Showing a good example—1 Timothy 4:12;
1 Peter 2:12

77. Shunning the wicked—Psalm 1:1; 2 Thessalonians 3:6

78. Sincerity—Psalm 15:1–2, 2 Chronicles 16:9;
2 Corinthians 1:12; 2:17

79. Spirit led—Romans 8:14

80. Steadfastness—Acts 2:42; Colossians 2:5

81. Submission to authority—Romans 13:1–7

82. Submission to injuries—Matthew 5:39–41;
    1 Corinthians 6:7

83. Sympathy with others—Galatians 6:2;
    1 Thessalonians 5:14

84. Temper control—Ephesians 4:26; James 1:19

85. Thoroughness—Colossians 3:22–24;
    Ecclesiastes 9:10

86. Thriftiness—Matthew 13:44; Matthew 25:21

87. Tolerance—1 Corinthians 12:25–27;
    Ephesians 4:12–13

88. Truthfulness—Proverbs 12:22; Ephesians 5:8–10

89. Undefiled—Psalm 119:1

90. Uprightness—1 Kings 3:6, Psalm 15:2

91. Vigilance—1 Peter 5:8

92. Virtue—2 Peter 1:3, 5; Proverbs 31:10–31

93. Visiting the afflicted—Matthew 25:36; James 1:27

94. Watchfulness—Luke 12:37

95. Wisdom—Proverbs 1:2–3; 4:7; 13:20

96. Zealous of good works—Titus 2:14; 3:8

LIST # 46
112 Wonderful Bible Memory Verses

Carrying God's Word in our hearts allows us to recall it when we most need it.

1. "Therefore you shall love the LORD your God, and keep His charge, His statutes, His Judgments, and His commandments always."—Deuteronomy 11:1

2. "Be strong and of good courage, do not fear nor be afraid of them; for the LORD your God, He is the One who goes with you. He will not leave you nor forsake you."—Deuteronomy 31:6

3. "This Book of the Law shall not depart from your mouth, but you shall meditate in it day and night, that you may observe to do according to all that is written in it. For then you will make your way prosperous, and then you will have good success."—Joshua 1:8

4. "Have I not commanded you? Be strong and of good courage; do not be afraid, nor be dismayed, for the LORD your God is with you wherever you go."—Joshua 1:9

5. "Blessed is the man who walks not in the counsel of the ungodly, nor stands in the path of sinners, nor sits in the seat of the scornful; but his delight is in the law of the LORD, and in His law he meditates day and night. He shall be like a tree planted by the rivers of water, that brings forth its fruit in its season, whose leaf also shall not wither; and whatever he does shall prosper."—Psalm 1:1–3

6. "Let the words of my mouth and the meditation of my heart be acceptable in Your sight, O Lord, my strength and my Redeemer."—Psalm 19:14

7. "The LORD is my shepherd; I shall not want. He makes me to lie down in green pastures; He leads me beside the still waters. He restores my soul; He leads me in the paths of righteousness for His name's sake. Yea, though I walk through the valley of the shadow of death, I will fear no evil; for You are with me; Your rod and Your staff, they comfort me. You prepare a table before me in the presence of my ene-mies; You anoint my head with oil; my cup runs over. Surely goodness and mercy shall follow me all the days of my life; and I will dwell in the house of the LORD Forever."—Psalm 23

8. "The LORD is my light and my salvation; whom shall I fear? The LORD is the strength of my life; of whom shall I be afraid?"—Psalm 27:1

9. "Oh, taste and see that the LORD is good; blessed is the man who trusts in Him!"—Psalm 34:8

10. "Keep your tongue from evil, and your lips from speaking deceit. Depart from evil and do good; seek peace and pursue it."—Psalm 34:13–14

11. "Delight yourself also in the LORD, and He shall give you the desires of your heart."—Psalm 37:4

12. "Commit your way to the LORD, trust also in Him, and He shall bring it to pass."—Psalm 37:5

13. "The steps of a good man are ordered by the LORD, and He delights in his way. Though he fall, he shall not be utterly cast down; for the LORD upholds him with His hand."—Psalm 37:23–24

14. "God is our refuge and strength, a very present help in trouble."—Psalm 46:1

15. "If I regard iniquity in my heart, the Lord will not hear."—Psalm 66:18

16. "Blessed be the Lord, who daily loads us with benefits, the God of our salvation!"—Psalm 68:19

17. "Oh, give thanks to the LORD, for He is good!" —Psalm 107:1

18. "How can a young man cleanse his way? By taking heed according to Your word. . . . Your word I have hidden in my heart, that I might not sin against You."—Psalm 119:9, 11

19. "Trust in the LORD with all your heart, and lean not on your own understanding; in all your ways acknowledge Him, and He shall direct your paths." —Proverbs 3:5–6

20. "The fear of the LORD is the beginning of wisdom, and the knowledge of the Holy One is understanding." —Proverbs 9:10

21. "In the multitude of words sin is not lacking, but he who restrains his lips is wise."—Proverbs 10:19

22. "The fruit of the righteous is a tree of life, and he who wins souls is wise."—Proverbs 11:30

23. "A soft answer turns away wrath, but a harsh word stirs up anger."—Proverbs 15:1

24. "Pride goes before destruction, and a haughty spirit before a fall."—Proverbs 16:18

25. "He who answers a matter before he hears it, it is folly and shame to him."—Proverbs 18:13

26. "The first one to plead his cause seems right, until his neighbor comes and examines him."
    —Proverbs 18:17

27. "The discretion of a man makes him slow to anger, and his glory is to overlook a transgression."
    —Proverbs 19:11

28. "Come now, and let us reason together," says the LORD, "though your sins are like scarlet, they shall be as white as snow; though they are red like crimson, they shall be as wool."—Isaiah 1:18

29. "You will keep him in perfect peace whose mind is stayed on You."—Isaiah 26:3

30. "The grass withers, the flower fades, but the word of our God stands forever."—Isaiah 40:8

31. "But those who wait on the LORD shall renew their strength; they shall mount up with wings like eagles, they shall run and not be weary, they shall walk and not faint."—Isaiah 40:31

32. "Thus says the LORD, your Redeemer, the Holy One of Israel: 'I am the LORD your God, who teaches you to profit, who leads you by the way you should go.'"
    —Isaiah 48:17

33. "Your words were found, and I ate them, and Your word was to me the joy and rejoicing of my heart; for I am called by Your name, O LORD God of hosts."
    —Jeremiah 15:16

34. "Then you will call upon Me and go and pray to Me, and I will listen to you. And you will seek Me and find Me, when you search for Me with all your heart."
    —Jeremiah 29:12–13

35. "Call to Me, and I will answer you, and show you great and mighty things, which you do not know." —Jeremiah 33:3

36. "'Bring all the tithes into the storehouse, that there may be food in My house, and try Me now in this,' says the LORD of hosts, 'If I will not open for you the windows of heaven and pour out for you such blessing that there will not be room enough to receive it.'" —Malachi 3:10

37. "Therefore whoever confesses Me before men, him I will also confess before My Father who is in heaven. But whoever denies Me before men, him I will also deny before My Father who is in heaven." —Matthew 10:32–33

38. "Come to Me, all you who labor and are heavy laden, and I will give you rest. Take My yoke upon you and learn from Me, for I am gentle and lowly in heart, and you will find rest for your souls. For My yoke is easy and My burden is light."—Matthew 11:28–30

39. "For what profit is it to a man if he gains the whole world, and loses his own soul? Or what will a man give in exchange for his soul?"—Matthew 16:26

40. "And whenever you stand praying, if you have anything against anyone, forgive him, that your Father in heaven may also forgive you your trespasses." —Mark 11:25

41. "But as many as received Him, to them He gave the right to become children of God, to those who believe in His name."—John 1:12

42. "For God so loved the world that He gave His only begotten Son, that whoever believes in Him should

not perish but have everlasting life."—John 3:16

43. "He who believes in the Son has everlasting life; and he who does not believe the Son shall not see life, but the wrath of God abides on him."—John 3:36

44. "But whoever drinks of the water that I shall give him will never thirst. But the water that I shall give him will become in him a fountain of water springing up into everlasting life."—John 4:14

45. "My sheep hear My voice, and I know them, and they follow Me. And I give them eternal life, and they shall never perish; neither shall anyone snatch them out of My hand. My Father, who has given them to Me, is greater than all; and no one is able to snatch them out of My Father's hand. I and My Father are one." —John 10:27–30

46. "Let not your heart be troubled; you believe in God, believe also in Me. In My Father's house are many mansions; if it were not so, I would have told you. I go to prepare a place for you."—John 14:1–2

47. "You did not choose Me, but I chose you and appointed you that you should go and bear fruit, and that your fruit should remain, that whatever you ask the Father in My name He may give you." —John 15:16

48. "But these are written that you may believe that Jesus is the Christ, the Son of God, and that believing you may have life in His name."—John 20:31

49. "But you shall receive power when the Holy Spirit has come upon you; and you shall be witnesses to Me in Jerusalem, and in all Judea and Samaria, and to the end of the earth."—Acts 1:8

50. "And it shall come to pass that whoever calls on the name of the LORD shall be saved."—Acts 2:21

51. "Nor is there salvation in any other, for there is no other name under heaven given among men by which we must be saved."—Acts 4:12

52. "For all have sinned and fall short of the glory of God."—Romans 3:23

53. "Therefore, having been justified by faith, we have peace with God through our Lord Jesus Christ."
    —Romans 5:1

54. "And not only that, but we also glory in tribulations, knowing that tribulation produces perseverance; and perseverance, character; and character, hope."
    —Romans 5:3–4

55. "For when we were still without strength, in due time Christ died for the ungodly."—Romans 5:6

56. "For the wages of sin is death, but the gift of God is eternal life in Christ Jesus our Lord."—Romans 6:23

57. "There is therefore now no condemnation to those who are in Christ Jesus, who do not walk according to the flesh, but according to the Spirit."—Romans 8:1

58. "The Spirit Himself bears witness with our spirit that we are children of God."—Romans 8:16

59. "And we know that all things work together for good to those who love God, to those who are the called according to His purpose."—Romans 8:28

60. "Who shall separate us from the love of Christ? Shall tribulation, or distress, or persecution, or famine, or nakedness, or peril, or sword? . . . For I am persuaded

that neither death nor life, nor angels nor principalities nor powers, nor things present nor things to come, nor height nor depth, nor any other created thing, shall be able to separate us from the love of God which is in Christ Jesus our Lord."
—Romans 8:35, 38–39

61. "That if you confess with your mouth the Lord Jesus and believe in your heart that God has raised Him from the dead, you will be saved. For with the heart one believes unto righteousness, and with the mouth confession is made unto salvation."
—Romans 10:9–10

62. "For whoever calls on the name of the LORD shall be saved."—Romans 10:13

63. "I beseech you therefore, brethren, by the mercies of God, that you present your bodies a living sacrifice, holy, acceptable to God, which is your reasonable service. And do not be conformed to this world, but be transformed by the renewing of your mind, that you may prove what is that good and acceptable and perfect will of God."—Romans 12:1–2

64. "For the kingdom of God is not eating and drinking, but righteousness and peace and joy in the Holy Spirit. . . . Therefore let us pursue the things which make for peace and the things by which one may edify another."—Romans 14:17, 19

65. "Or do you not know that your body is the temple of the Holy Spirit who is in you, whom you have from God, and you are not your own? For you were bought at a price; therefore glorify God in your body and in your spirit, which are God's."—1 Corinthians 6:19–20

66. "No temptation has overtaken you except such as is common to man; but God is faithful, who will not allow you to be tempted beyond what you are able, but with the temptation will also make the way of escape, that you may be able to bear it."—1 Corinthians 10:13

67. "Therefore, my beloved brethren, be steadfast, immovable, always abounding in the work of the Lord, knowing that your labor is not in vain in the Lord."—1 Corinthians 15:58

68. "Blessed be the God and Father of our Lord Jesus Christ, the Father of mercies and God of all comfort, who comforts us in all our tribulation, that we may be able to comfort those who are in any trouble, with the comfort with which we ourselves are comforted by God. For as the sufferings of Christ abound in us, so our consolation also abounds through Christ."
—2 Corinthians 1:3–5

69. "Now thanks be to God who always leads us in triumph in Christ, and through us diffuses the fragrance of His knowledge in every place."—2 Corinthians 2:14

70. "Therefore, if anyone is in Christ, he is a new creation; old things have passed away; behold, all things have become new."—2 Corinthians 5:17

71. "Now then, we are ambassadors for Christ, as though God were pleading through us: we implore you on Christ's behalf, be reconciled to God."
—2 Corinthians 5:20

72. "For He made Him who knew no sin to be sin for us, that we might become the righteousness of God in Him."—2 Corinthians 5:21

73. "And He said to me, 'My grace is sufficient for you, for My strength is made perfect in weakness.'"
—2 Corinthians 12:9

74. "I have been crucified with Christ; it is no longer I who live, but Christ lives in me; and the life which I now live in the flesh I live by faith in the Son of God, who loved me and gave Himself for me."—Galatians 2:20

75. "I say then: 'Walk in the Spirit, and you shall not fulfill the lust of the flesh.'"—Galatians 5:16

76. "Do not be deceived, God is not mocked; for whatever a man sows, that he will also reap. For he who sows to his flesh will of the flesh reap corruption, but he who sows to the Spirit will of the Spirit reap everlasting life."—Galatians 6:7–8

77. "And let us not grow weary while doing good, for in due season we shall reap if we do not lose heart. Therefore, as we have opportunity, let us do good to all, especially to those who are of the household of faith."—Galatians 6:8–10

78. "Blessed be the God and Father of our Lord Jesus Christ, who has blessed us with every spiritual blessing in the heavenly places in Christ."—Ephesians 1:3

79. "For by grace you have been saved through faith, and that not of yourselves; it is the gift of God, not of works, lest anyone should boast."—Ephesians 2:8–9

80. "For we are His workmanship, created in Christ Jesus for good works, which God prepared beforehand that we should walk in them."—Ephesians 2:10

81. "Now to Him who is able to do exceedingly abundantly above all that we ask or think, according to the

power that works in us."—Ephesians 3:20

82. "Let all bitterness, wrath, anger, clamor, and evil speaking be put away from you, with all malice. And be kind to one another, tenderhearted, forgiving one another, even as God in Christ forgave you."
—Ephesians 4:31–32

83. "Finally, my brethren, be strong in the Lord and in the power of His might. Put on the whole armor of God, that you may be able to stand against the wiles of the devil."—Ephesians 6:10–11

84. "Being confident of this very thing, that He who has begun a good work in you will complete it until the day of Jesus Christ."—Philippians 1:6

85. "That I may know Him and the power of His resurrection, and the fellowship of His sufferings, being conformed to His death."—Philippians 3:10

86. "Finally, brethren, whatever things are true, whatever things are noble, whatever things are just, whatever things are pure, whatever things are lovely, whatever things are of good report, if there is any virtue and if there is anything praiseworthy—meditate on these things."—Philippians 4:8–9

87. "Not that I speak in regard to need, for I have learned in whatever state I am, to be content."
—Philippians 4:11

88. "And my God shall supply all your need according to His riches in glory by Christ Jesus."—Philippians 4:19

89. "For in Him dwells all the fullness of the Godhead bodily; and you are complete in Him, who is the head of all principality and power."—Colossians 2:9–10

90. "And whatever you do in word or deed, do all in the name of the Lord Jesus, giving thanks to God the Father through Him."—Colossians 3:17

91. "And whatever you do, do it heartily, as to the Lord and not to men, knowing that from the Lord you will receive the reward of the inheritance; for you serve the Lord Christ."—Colossians 3:23–24

92. "Walk in wisdom toward those who are outside, redeeming the time. Let your speech always be with grace, seasoned with salt, that you may know how you ought to answer each one."—Colossians 4:5–6

93. "Rejoice always, pray without ceasing, in everything give thanks; for this is the will of God in Christ Jesus for you."—1 Thessalonians 5:16–18

94. "Be diligent to present yourself approved to God, a worker who does not need to be ashamed, rightly dividing the word of truth."—2 Timothy 2:15

95. "All Scripture is given by inspiration of God, and is profitable for doctrine, for reproof, for correction, for instruction in righteousness, that the man of God may be complete, thoroughly equipped for every good work."—2 Timothy 3:16–17

96. "Not by works of righteousness which we have done, but according to His mercy He saved us, through the washing of regeneration and renewing of the Holy Spirit, who He poured out on us abundantly through Jesus Christ our Savior."—Titus 3:5–6

97. "Let us therefore come boldly to the throne of grace, that we may obtain mercy and find grace to help in time of need."—Hebrews 4:16

98. "But without faith it is impossible to please Him, for he who comes to God must believe that He is, and that He is a rewarder of those who diligently seek Him." —Hebrews 11:6

99. "If any of you lacks wisdom, let him ask of God, who gives to all liberally and without reproach, and it will be given to him. But let him ask in faith, with no doubting, for he who doubts is like a wave of the sea driven and tossed by the wind."—James 1:5–6

100. "Blessed is the man who endures temptation; for when he has been approved, he will receive the crown of life which the Lord has promised to those who love Him."—James 1:12

101. "But be doers of the word, and not hearers only, deceiving yourselves."—James 1:22

102. "Therefore submit to God. Resist the devil and he will flee from you."—James 4:7

103. "Blessed be the God and Father of our Lord Jesus Christ, who according to His abundant mercy has begotten us again to a living hope through the resur- rection of Jesus Christ from the dead, to an inheri- tance incorruptible and undefiled and that does not fade away, reserved in heaven for you." —1 Peter 1:3–4

104. "As newborn babes, desire the pure milk of the word, that you may grow thereby."—1 Peter 2:2

105. "But sanctify the Lord God in your hearts, and always be ready to give a defense to everyone who asks you a reason for the hope that is in you, with meekness and fear."—1 Peter 3:15

106. "Therefore humble yourselves under the mighty hand of God, that He may exalt you in due time, casting all your care upon Him, for He cares for you."
—1 Peter 5:6–7

107. "As His divine power has given to us all things that pertain to life and godliness, through the knowledge of Him who called us by glory and virtue."
—2 Peter 1:3

108. "If we confess our sins, He is faithful and just to forgive us our sins and to cleanse us from all unrighteousness."—1 John 1:9

109. "Do not love the world or the things in the world. If anyone loves the world, the love of the Father is not in him."—1 John 2:15

110. "And this is the testimony: that God has given us eternal life, and this life is in His Son. He who has the Son has life; he who does not have the Son of God does not have life."—1 John 5:11–12

111. "These things I have written to you who believe in the name of the Son of God, that you may know that you have eternal life, and that you may continue to believe in the name of the Son of God."—1 John 5:13

112. "Behold, I stand at the door and knock. If anyone hears My voice and opens the door, I will come in to him and dine with him, and he with Me."
—Revelation 3:20

▄LIST #47
78 Interesting Subjects

Here are 78 of the fascinating, diverse subjects found in the Bible, along with a series of over 350 references.

1. Assurance of Salvation
    - John 5:24; 6:37; 10:27–30; 20:31
    - Romans 8:16, 31, 35–39
    - Hebrews 13:5
    - 1 John 5:11–13

2. Battle of Armageddon
    - Revelation 14:14–20; 16:16

3. Beatitudes
    - Matthew 5:3–12
    - Luke 6:20–26

4. Christian Fellowship
    - Psalm 122:1, 9
    - Matthew 18:20
    - John 13:34
    - Acts 2:42, 46
    - 1 Corinthians 1:9
    - Hebrews 10:24–25
    - 1 John 1:3, 7

5. Christian's Armor
    - Ephesians 6:11–18

6. Crowns
   - 1 Corinthians 9:25
   - 1 Thessalonians 2:19–20
   - 2 Timothy 4:8
   - James 1:12
   - 1 Peter 5:2–4
   - Revelation 2:10

7. Danger
   - Psalms 23:4; 32:7; 34:7, 17, 19; 91:1–2, 11; 121:1–8
   - Isaiah 43:2
   - Romans 14:8

8. Death
   - Psalms 23:4; 116:15
   - Romans 14:8
   - 2 Corinthians 5:1
   - Philippians 1:21
   - 1 Thessalonians 5:9–10
   - 2 Timothy 4:7–8
   - Hebrews 9:27

9. Deity of Christ
   - Matthew 26:63–64
   - John 1:1–14, 18; 10:30; 14:9; 16:15; 17:10; 20:28
   - Romans 9:5
   - Colossians 1:15–19; 2:9
   - Titus 2:13
   - Hebrews 1:3, 8
   - 1 John 5:20

10. Doubtful Practices
    - Romans 14:1–23
    - 1 Corinthians 8:9, 13
    - Philippians 2:15
    - Colossians 3:2, 5–10, 17
    - 1 Thessalonians 5:22
    - Titus 2:12–14
    - James 4:4
    - 1 John 2:15–17

11. External Pressures
    - Joshua 1:9
    - Psalm 37:5
    - Romans 8:28
    - 2 Corinthians 12:9
    - 1 Peter 5:7
    - 1 John 5:4–5

12. Faith
    - Romans 4:3; 10:17
    - Ephesians 2:8–9
    - Hebrews 11:1, 6; 12:2
    - James 1:3–6
    - 1 Peter 1:7

13. Forgiving Others
    - Proverbs 18:19
    - Mark 11:25–26
    - Luke 17:3–4
    - Ephesians 4:32
    - Colossians 3:13

14. Fruit of the Spirit
    - Galatians 5:22–23

15. Generosity
    - 1 Chronicles 29:9
    - Psalm 37:21
    - Luke 6:38
    - Matthew 5:42
    - Proverbs 3:9–10
    - 2 Corinthians 9:6–7

16. God's Care
    - Psalms 31:19–20; 34:17–19; 91:1–2
    - Nahum 1:7
    - Ephesians 3:20
    - Philippians 4:19
    - 1 Peter 5:7
    - 1 John 4:16
    - Jude 1:24

17. Golden Rule
    - Matthew 7:12
    - Luke 6:31

18. Great White Throne
    - Revelation 20:11–15

19. Growing Spiritually
    - Ephesians 3:17–19
    - Colossians 1:9–11; 3:16
    - 1 Timothy 4:15
    - 2 Timothy 2:15

- 1 Peter 2:2
- 2 Peter 1:5–8; 3:18

20. Guidance
    - Psalm 32:8
    - Isaiah 30:21; 58:11
    - Luke 1:79
    - John 16:13

21. Help and Care
    - 2 Chronicles 16:9
    - Psalms 34:7; 37:5, 24; 55:22; 91:4
    - Isaiah 50:9; 54:17
    - Hebrews 4:16; 13:5–6
    - 1 Peter 5:7

22. Holy Spirit
    - Acts 5:3–4
    - 1 Corinthians 3:16; 6:19; 12:4–6
    - 2 Corinthians 13:14

23. Honesty
    - Romans 13:13
    - 1 Thessalonians 4:11–12
    - Hebrews 13:18
    - 1 Peter 2:11–12

24. Humility
    - Proverbs 22:4
    - Micah 6:8
    - Acts 20:19
    - Romans 12:3

- Philippians 2:3–4
- 1 Peter 5:5–6

25. Husbands and Fathers
    - Genesis 18:19
    - Proverbs 23:13–14
    - 1 Corinthians 7:3–4, 14
    - Ephesians 5:23–29; 6:4

26. Jesus—Savior of the World
    - Matthew 1:21
    - Luke 19:10
    - John 3:16; 14:6
    - Acts 4:12
    - Romans 5:8
    - Ephesians 1:7
    - 1 John 5:12

27. Judgment Seat of Christ
    - Matthew 6:2–4; 25:14–30
    - Luke 19:11–27
    - Romans 14:10–12
    - 1 Corinthians 3:9–15
    - 2 Timothy 4:8

28. Kingdom Age
    - Isaiah 11:6–9; 14:7–8; 25:8–9
    - Revelation 20:1–6

29. Lake of Fire
    - Revelation 19:20; 20:10, 14–15

30. Liberty
   - John 8:32, 36
   - Romans 6:6–7, 17–22; 7:6; 8:2; 14:1–23
   - 1 Corinthians 8:1–13
   - Galatians 2:21; 5:1, 13–14

31. Living the Christian Life
   - Psalm 119:9–11
   - John 15:7
   - 2 Corinthians 5:17
   - Colossians 2:6
   - 1 Peter 2:2
   - 1 John 1:7

32. Lord's Prayer
   - Matthew 6:9–15
   - Luke 11:1–13

33. Lord's Supper
   - Matthew 26:26–29
   - Luke 22:19–20
   - 1 Corinthians 11:23–26

34. Lordship
   - Luke 6:46
   - Romans 6:13–16; 10:9–10; 12:1–2
   - 1 Corinthians 6:19–20
   - Philippians 2:9–11

35. Love
   - John 3:16; 15:9–14

- Romans 5:8; 8:35–39
- 1 Corinthians 13:1–13
- 1 John 3:1

36. Lying
- Proverbs 6:16–19; 12:22
- Colossians 3:9

37. Mark of the Beast
- Revelation 13:1–18

38. Marriage Supper of the Lamb
- Revelation 19:7–10

39. Man's Need of Salvation
- Isaiah 64:6
- Romans 3:10, 23; 5:12; 6:23
- Hebrews 9:27
- 1 John 1:10

40. National Responsibilities
- Psalm 33:12
- Romans 13:1–7
- 1 Timothy 2:1–3
- 1 Peter 2:13–17

41. New Heaven and Earth
- Isaiah 65:17–25
- Revelation 21–22:15

42. Occupation
- Genesis 2:15
- Proverbs 14:23

- Ecclesiastes 9:10
- Romans 12:11–13
- Ephesians 4:28
- 2 Thessalonians 3:10–12

43. One Hundred and Forty–Four Thousand
    - Revelation 7:4–8

44. Paradise and Hades
    - Numbers 16:33
    - Luke 16:22–31; 23:43

45. Parents and Children
    - Exodus 20:12
    - Proverbs 1:8–9; 6:20–23; 23:22–26; 28:7
    - Ephesians 6:1–4
    - Colossians 3:20–21
    - 1 Timothy 4:12; 5:4

46. Persecution
    - Matthew 5:10–11; 10:22
    - Acts 5:41; 9:16
    - Romans 8:17
    - 2 Timothy 3:12
    - Hebrews 11:25
    - James 1:2–4
    - 1 Peter 2:20

47. Plan of Salvation
    - Isaiah 55:7
    - John 1:12; 3:3; 5:24

- Romans 10:9–10, 13
- Ephesians 2:8–9
- Titus 3:5–7
- 1 John 5:11–13
- Revelation 3:20

48. Power over Satan
    - James 4:7
    - 1 John 4:4

49. Praise and Gratitude
    - Deuteronomy 8:10
    - 1 Samuel 12:24
    - 2 Chronicles 20:7–30
    - Psalms 43:1–4; 50:23; 51:15; 63:2–7; 100:4; 107:8; 150:1–6
    - Ephesians 5:18–20
    - Philippians 4:4–6
    - Colossians 3:15–17
    - 1 Thessalonians 5:18
    - Hebrews 13:15
    - 1 Peter 1:6–9

50. Prayer
    - Psalms 10:17; 18:3; 86:5, 7; 145:18
    - Jeremiah 33:3
    - Joel 2:32
    - Matthew 7:7–8; 21:22
    - John 14:13–14; 15:7
    - Romans 10:9–13

- Ephesians 6:18
- Hebrews 4:14–16
- James 5:16
- 1 John 5:14–15

51. Provision
   - Psalm 23:1–6; 34:10; 37:3–4; 84:11
   - Isaiah 58:11
   - Matthew 6:33
   - 2 Corinthians 9:8
   - Ephesians 3:20
   - 1 Peter 1:3–5
   - 2 Peter 1:3–4

52. Purity
   - Philippians 2:14–15
   - 1 Timothy 5:22
   - James 3:17; 4:8
   - 1 John 3:3

53. Rapture
   - 1 Corinthians 15:51–57
   - 1 Thessalonians 4:13–18

54. Return of Christ
   - Luke 21:34–36
   - Acts 1:11
   - 1 Thessalonians 4:13–18
   - Titus 2:13
   - 2 Peter 3:8–14
   - 1 John 3:2–3

55. Rewards
    - 1 Corinthians 3:11–15
    - Ephesians 5:27; 6:8
    - 2 Thessalonians 2:14
    - 2 Timothy 4:8
    - 1 John 3:1–2
    - Jude 1:24

56. Satan
    - Isaiah 14:12–15
    - Ezekiel 28:12–19
    - James 4:7
    - 2 Peter 2:9
    - 1 John 4:4

57. Seal Judgments
    - Revelation 6:1–7:17

58. Self-Image
    - 1 Samuel 16:7
    - Psalms 138:8; 139:14–16
    - Philippians 1:6

59. Self-Control
    - Proverbs 4:23–26
    - Romans 13:14
    - 1 Corinthians 9:25; 10:13; 16:13

60. Signs of the Times
    - Isaiah 35:1–2
    - Daniel 11:40; 12:4

- Ezekiel 36:30; 38:14–16; 44:1–2
- Matthew 24:7, 15
- Luke 21:25
- 2 Thessalonians 2:4
- James 5:1–3

61. Social Events and Signs
   - Genesis 6:5; 13:13
   - Deuteronomy 28:63–67
   - Ezekiel 34:11–13; 36:24; 38:1–39:29
   - Zechariah 12:2–3
   - Matthew 24:6, 9–10; 12:37–39
   - Mark 7:21, 23
   - Luke 17:28–29; 21:24–25
   - Revelation 9:13–21; 21:8; 22:15

62. Religious Signs
   - Daniel 8:23–25; 11:36–45
   - Joel 2:28–29
   - Matthew 24:5, 11, 13–14, 34
   - 1 Timothy 4:1
   - 2 Timothy 4:3–4
   - 2 Peter 2:1–2; 3:3–4
   - Revelation 13:1–18

63. Social Responsibilities
   - Proverbs 19:17
   - Matthew 5:13–15; 10:42
   - Luke 3:10–11

- Galatians 6:1–5
- 1 John 3:17–18

64. Sorrow
- Job 5:17–18
- Proverbs 23:29–35
- Isaiah 53:4
- Matthew 11:28–30
- John 16:22
- 2 Corinthians 1:3–5; 4:9–13; 6:10
- 1 Thessalonians 4:13
- 1 Peter 1:7; 4:12–13
- Revelation 21:4

65. Spiritual Gifts
- Romans 12:6–8
- 1 Corinthians 12:1–14:40
- Ephesians 4:11–12
- 1 Peter 4:10

66. Strength
- Deuteronomy 33:25
- Psalms 27:14; 28:7
- Isaiah 40:29, 31; 41:10
- 2 Corinthians 12:9
- Philippians 4:13

67. Study
- Psalms 19:7–11; 119:9, 11, 18
- Acts 20:32

- 2 Timothy 3:15–17
- Hebrews 4:12
- 1 Peter 2:2

68. Ten Commandments
- Exodus 20:1–26

69. Those Who Haven't Heard
- John 6:45; 12:32; 16:8
- Romans 1:19–20; 2:15, 18

70. Tribulation Period
- Daniel 9:24–27
- Revelation 11:2–3; 13:5

71. Trumpet Judgments
- Revelation 8:1–9:21

72. Trusting
- Psalms 5:11; 18:2; 37:5
- Proverbs 3:5–6
- Isaiah 12:2; 26:3–4

73. Two Witnesses
- Revelation 11:3–12

74. Vial Judgments
- Revelation 16:1–21 (KJV)

75. Victory
- 2 Chronicles 32:8
- Romans 8:37
- 1 Corinthians 15:57
- 2 Corinthians 2:14

- 1 John 5:4
- Revelation 3:5; 21:7

76. Witchcraft
- Exodus 22:18
- Deuteronomy 18:10
- Micah 5:12
- Malachi 3:5
- Galatians 5:20
- Revelation 21:8; 22:15

77. Witnessing
- Psalm 66:16
- Proverbs 11:30
- Matthew 5:16
- Mark 5:19
- Luke 24:48
- Acts 1:8
- Romans 1:16
- 2 Corinthians 5:18–20
- 1 Peter 3:15; 4:11

78. Wives and Mothers
- Proverbs 12:4; 14:1; 22:6, 15; 29:15; 31:10–31
- Ephesians 5:22–24
- 1 Timothy 3:11
- Titus 2:3–5
- 1 Peter 3:1–6

▖LIST #48
125 Counseling Helps from the Bible

If you are involved in any type of counseling—whether lay or professional, this list will be helpful with over 550 references on 125 different topics.

1. Abortion
   - God forms the baby in the womb.—Jeremiah 1:1–5
   - God knits together the baby.—Job 10:8–12
   - Children are God's gift.—Psalm 127:3–5
   - God forms the baby and ordains each day.
     —Psalm 139:1–24
   - God makes and forms the baby.—Isaiah 44:2

2. Abusive Behavior
   - Give preference to one another.—Romans 12:10
   - Be at peace and do not seek revenge.
     —Romans 12:18–19
   - Behave so as to glorify God in everything.
     —1 Corinthians 10:31
   - Don't repay evil with evil.—1 Thessalonians 5:15
   - Anger does not achieve God's righteousness.
     —James 1:20

3. Accountability
   - God judges unfaithfulness.—Joshua 7:1–15
   - Doing your own thing brings God's wrath.
     —Judges 6:1–16

- One day God will judge every act.
  —Ecclesiastes 12:13–14

- Everyone will give an account of how they've lived.—Romans 14:1–22

4. Adultery

  - Adultery is turning from the first love to another.
    —Isaiah 1:1–31

  - Adultery is forsaking the Lord.—Hosea 1:1–11

  - Here are Jesus's thoughts on adultery.
    —Matthew 5:27–32

  - Jesus teaches about adultery and divorce.
    —Luke 16:16–18

  - Jesus tells the adulterous person what to do.
    —John 8:1–11

5. Advice

  - Learn to get all the advice you can.
    —Proverbs 1:1–9

  - Listen to the advice of your parents.
    —Proverbs 6:20–24

  - Here are practical examples of listening to advice.—Proverbs 19:1–21

  - This is advice that will change your life.
    —Mark 10:17–31

6. Affections

  - It is from our affections that the issues of life come.—Proverbs 4:23–27

7. Alcoholism

  - Being intoxicated is not wise.—Proverbs 20:1

- These are the negative results of drinking.
  —Proverbs 23:29–35

- Being with a company of drinkers can corrupt.
  —1 Corinthians 15:33

- Drinking can enslave a person.—2 Peter 2:19

8. Anger

- It's wise to be slow to anger.—Proverbs 14:29

- Gentle words turn away wrath and anger.
  —Proverbs 15:1

- Get rid of your anger; it could lead to murder.
  —Matthew 5:21–26

- True love is not easily provoked to anger.
  —1 Corinthians 13:4–5

- Do not let the sun go down on your anger.
  —Ephesians 4:26–32

- Learn to become slow to anger.—James 1:19–20

- An angry tongue is sparked by hell's fire.
  —James 3:6

9. Anxiety

- In God's presence there is joy.—Psalm 16:11

- Don't get upset when the wicked seem to prosper.
  —Psalm 37:1, 7

- Hope in God will help your countenance.
  —Psalm 43:5

- Pleasing the Lord brings peace.—Proverbs 16:7

- Don't fear; don't be anxious. God is with you.
  —Isaiah 41:10

- Don't be anxious about your daily needs.
  —Matthew 6:31–34

- Conquer anxiety with a attitude of thanksgiving.
  —Philippians 4:6–9, 19

- Give your load of anxiety to God.—1 Peter 5:7

10. Arguments

- Run from arguments and pursue righteousness.
  —Proverbs 15:1–9

- Overlooking personal offenses pays off.
  —Proverbs 19:11

- Stirring up arguments has severe consequences.
  —Proverbs 26:17–28

- Don't grumble or get into a rumble.
  —Philippians 2:12–18

- Foolish controversies and disputes are unprofitable.
  —Titus 3:1–11

11. Attitude

- Develop the attitude of a servant leader.
  —Philippians 2:5–11

- God's peace comes from changing your attitude.
  —Philippians 4:4–9

12. Backsliding

- Turning from God soon brings trouble.
  —Deuteronomy 8:10–20

- Keep your hand to the plow.—Luke 9:57–62

- Try to help turn another away from destruction.
  —James 5:15–20

13. Bad Company

- Those who do evil want you to join them.
  —Proverbs 2:12–19

- The road to bad morals starts with bad company.
  —1 Corinthians 15:33

14. Belief

    - Your belief will determine your destiny.
      —Romans 10:5–13

    - Live your life according to your beliefs.
      —James 2:14–24

15. Bereavement

    - God will not fail in your time of need.
      —Deuteronomy 31:8

    - The shepherd prepares your path.—Psalm 23:1–6

    - All others may leave but God will stay with you.
      —Psalm 27:10

    - God will comfort you in your affliction.
      —Psalm 119:50

16. Bitterness

    - Bitterness poisons everyone it touches.
      —Hebrews 12:14–17

    - We love God by forgiving others.—1 John 3:11–24

17. Blaming Others

    - When we blame others we reject responsibility.
      —Genesis 3:11–13

    - Aaron made the golden calf but blamed the
      people.—Exodus 32:21–22

    - The foolish blamer rages against the Lord.
      —Proverbs 19:1–3

    - We point out others' faults and ignore our own.
      —Matthew 7:1–5

161

18. Burdens

  - Learn to carry the wheelbarrow load for others.
    —Romans 12:13

  - Bear your brother's burdens.—Galatians 6:2

19. Child Abuse

  - Do not provoke your children.—Ephesians 6:4

  - Don't crush your child's spirit.—Colossians 3:21

20. Christian Character

  - Overcome evil by doing the right thing.
    —Romans 12:1–2, 9–21

  - The fruit of the Spirit is proof of godly character.
    —Galatians 5:16–17, 22–23

  - Put on a whole new wardrobe of godly living.
    —Ephesians 4:17–32

  - This is a whole new way of life.—Colossians 3:1–17

21. Choices

  - Choosing the right path is very important.
    —Proverbs 1:1–19

  - A wise man drinks at the fountain of life.
    —Proverbs 13:1–16

  - Following Jesus brings a brand-new adventure.
    —Matthew 9:9–13

22. Comfort

  - This is the honest cry of a man in pain.
    —Job 16:1–22

  - My cup will surely run over with God's blessings.
    —Psalm 23

  - The Lord's loving-kindness never fails.
    —Lamentations 3:21–26

- God will comfort those who mourn.—Matthew 5:4
- God will give rest to the weary.—Matthew 11:28–30
- The Father will send His Comforter to you.
  —John 14:16–18
- Proven character comes from troubles.
  —Romans 5:3–5
- Help others as you have been helped.
  —2 Corinthians 1:3–5
- Eternal comfort and hope are priceless gifts.
  —2 Thessalonians 2:16–17

23. Complaining

- Do everything without whining and griping.
  —Philippians 2:12–18

24. Compromise

- Compromise leads to slavery.—Romans 6:15–18
- Learn to walk in the way of wisdom.
  —Ephesians 5:1–21
- Give up the former lustful life.—1 Peter 1:14–16
- Let go of the things of the world.—1 John 2:15–17

25. Confidence

- Be confident in the midst of trouble.—Psalm 27:3
- Keep your foot out of the trap.—Proverbs 3:26
- Fearing God is the starting place.—Proverbs 14:26
- Strength comes from quietness and trust.
  —Isaiah 30:15
- One day we will be rewarded.—Colossians 3:24
- Jesus Christ gives us access to God.
  —Ephesians 3:11–12

- God is not through with us yet.—Philippians 1:6
- Great rewards follow endurance.
  —Hebrews 10:35–36
- You have a new position in a royal priesthood.
  —1 Peter 2:9

26. Conflicts

- Selfishness is the starter seed for conflict.
  —James 4:1–12

27. Conscience

- Your conscience gives you either peace or pain.
  —Proverbs 28:13–18
- A clear conscience is a good pillow for sleep.
  —Acts 23:1
- Learn to have a blameless conscience.
  —Acts 24:16
- Share your faith with a clear conscience.
  —1 Timothy 3:8–9
- Be cleansed from an evil conscience.
  —Hebrews 10:21–22
- Good behavior brings a good conscience.
  —1 Peter 3:16

28. Criticism

- Learn to give up the judgmental spirit.
  —Matthew 7:1–5
- Don't be the person to bring on criticism.
  —Luke 17:1–10
- Don't bring dishonor to the cause of Christ.
  —Galatians 5:13–26

29. Deceit

   - God is not fooled by our behavior.
     —Exodus 20:1–21

30. Decision Making

   - Who are you going to serve?—Joshua 24:15

   - In every thing you do—glorify God.
     —1 Corinthians 10:31

   - Do all in the name of Jesus.—Colossians 3:17

   - Fix your eyes on Jesus and His goal for you.
     —Hebrews 12:1–2

   - Ask God for wisdom.—James 1:5

31. Demonic Deception

   - Satan is an angel of light.—2 Corinthians 11:3–15

   - Beware of the same thing that caused Satan's
     fall.—1 Timothy 3:6–7

   - Flee from the doctrine of devils.—1 Timothy 4:1

   - This is the secret for resisting the devil.—James 4:7

   - Someone is searching for your weakness.
     —1 Peter 5:8

32. Depression

   - Elijah dealt with depression.—1 Kings 19:1–9

   - Escape from the pit of despair.—Psalm 42:1–11

33. Desires

   - Learn to hate evil.—Psalm 97:1–12

34. Difficulties

   - God is not caught off guard by your troubles.
     —Romans 8:28

- Learn to recount God's blessings in your life.
  —2 Corinthians 4:17

- Christ is our example of enduring suffering.
  —Hebrews 5:8

- Submit to the bridle and the bit.—Hebrews 12:7–11

- God's correction demonstrates His love.
  —Revelation 3:19

35. Disagreement

- Settle your disagreements before worshiping.
  —Matthew 5:23–25

- Learn to follow God's plan for disagreement.
  —Matthew 18:15–22

- Follow the example of being unified.—John 17:21–23

- Stay clear of those who cause division.
  —Romans 16:17

- Paul begs for your cooperation against contention.
  —1 Corinthians 1:10

- Stop the division now.—1 Corinthians 12:25

- Move from bitterness to forgiveness.
  —Ephesians 4:31–32

36. Disappointment

- Hoping in God relieves disappointment.
  —Psalm 43:5

- Dump your disappointment.—Psalm 55:22

- Learn to get the big picture.—Psalm 126:6

- The peace of Jesus is a sure cure.—John 14:27

- Here's a realistic look at life's disappointments.
  —2 Corinthians 4:8–10

37. Discernment
- Ask God for discernment. —1 Kings 3:9
- Look inward before you look outward. —Matthew 7:1–12
- We are not all the same. —Romans 14:1–5
- Hold on to the proven good. —1 Thessalonians 5:21–22
- The secret to getting rid of doubt is faith. —James 1:2–8
- Test the spirits to see if they are true. —1 John 4:1

38. Discouragement
- God will never leave you. —Joshua 1:9
- Sometimes the answer is not yes or no but wait. —Psalm 27:14
- Look up instead of down. —Psalm 43:5
- Find peace in the midst of trouble. —John 14:1–3, 27
- There is good news of victory. —John 16:33
- Learn to care for others in the midst of trouble. —John 19:25–27
- This world is not your home. —Colossians 1:5
- Boldness is sometimes the answer. —Hebrews 4:16
- Each season has a reason. —1 Peter 1:3–9
- Maybe you haven't been asking. —1 John 5:14
- There is a glorious day coming. —Revelation 22:1–4

39. Dishonesty
- What do you think God thinks of dishonesty? —Proverbs 20:23–30

40. Disobedience

- Passing the buck of responsibility is still popular.
  —Genesis 3:1–24

- God is gravely displeased with disobedience.
  —1 Chronicles 13:1–14

41. Divisions

- Don't think of yourself as better than another.
  —1 Chronicles 4:6–13

42. Divorce and Remarriage

- Moses talks about divorce.—Deuteronomy 24:1–4

- God really hates divorce.—Malachi 2:15–16

- Jesus clarifies the law of Moses.
  —Matthew 5:31–32

- Jesus talks about the hardened heart.
  —Matthew 19:8–9

- Jesus deals with a hot issue.—Mark 10:2–12

- Jesus addresses divorce and adultery.—Luke 16:18

- The process is laid out in detail.
  —1 Corinthians 7:10–15

43. Drinking and Drug Abuse

- Drinking can bring serious repercussions.
  —Proverbs 20:1

- Associating with drinkers can lead to poverty.
  —Proverbs 23:19–21

- Drinking will distract you from looking for Jesus.
  —Luke 21:34

- Always practice self-control.—Romans 6:12

- Do not walk the wrong way.—Romans 13:13

- Is what you are doing glorifying to God?
  —1 Corinthians 6:15, 19–20
- Let the Spirit of God be your intoxication.
  —Ephesians 5:15–20

44. Encouragement

- Take heart! We can trust the Lord for everything.
  —1 Thessalonians 5:1–28
- Our faith is as pure gold. —1 Peter 1:1–13

45. Enthusiasm

- Put your heart and soul into living for Jesus.
  —Colossians 3:18–25

46. Envy

- Get your eyes off what is not yours.
  —Deuteronomy 5:21
- This is an example of envy taken to the extreme.
  —1 Kings 21:1–29

47. Eternal Life

- What is truly valuable to you in the end?
  —Luke 18:18–30
- From start to finish—how do I get eternal life?
  —John 3:1–36
- God starts and finishes the process.
  —John 6:60–71
- Jesus is praying for each one of His own.
  —John 17:1–26
- Salvation is guaranteed for those who will believe.
  —1 John 5:1–13

48. Faults

- Look at your own faults.—Matthew 7:1–5
- Surrender every part of your life to the Lord.
—Ephesians 4:1–16

49. Fear

- You never have to fear when the Lord is near.
—Joshua 1:1–18
- Where does strength to face fears come from?
—Psalm 27:1
- With God as your foundation—who can shake it?
—Psalm 56:11
- Here's a place to hide when you are afraid.
—Psalm 91:1–6
- You always have protection.—Psalm 121:1–8
- Firm footing is guaranteed in shaky times.
—Proverbs 3:25–26
- The key is where you focus your thoughts.
—Proverbs 29:25
- Comfort is near when you are afraid.—Isaiah 51:12
- Are you looking for peace? Look no further.
—John 14:27
- Fear not—God is in absolute control.
—Romans 8:28–29, 31, 35–39
- This is the peace process in detail.
—Philippians 4:8–9, 19
- God gives three things to combat fear.
—2 Timothy 1:7
- Fight fear by demonstrating love.—1 John 4:18
- Here is the power to fight away fear.
—Jude 1:24–25

50. Feelings

- Move away from feelings and trust facts.
  —Romans 5:9–21

51. Financial Difficulties

- Who owns the money?—Psalm 24:1

- This is a guarantee for life.—Psalm 37:25

- He owns the cattle on a thousand hills.
  —Psalm 50:10, 14–15

- What happens when you borrow money?
  —Proverbs 22:7

- This is the greatest investment possible.
  —Matthew 6:19–34

- With money comes responsibility.
  —1 Corinthians 4:2

- Needs or desires and wants? Which is it?
  —Philippians 4:19

- Money itself is not evil.—1 Timothy 6:9–10

52. Foolishness

- This is the ultimate in foolishness.—Psalm 14:1–7

- Here is the secret for dealing with foolishness.
  —Proverbs 9:1–18

- Why do people become foolish?
  —1 Corinthians 2:6–16

53. Forgiveness

- Forgiveness starts with a broken spirit.
  —Psalm 51:1–19

- To be forgiven—start by forgiving others.
  —Matthew 6:5–15

- We should always forgive.—Matthew 18:21–35
- How do we get revenge?—Romans 12:1–21
- How do we obtain forgiveness?—1 John 1:1–10

54. Friendship

- A friend does not give up during times of trouble.
  —Proverbs 17:1–28
- A friend stays closer than a brother.
  —Proverbs 18:24
- Christians are known by the way they love.
  —John 13:35
- Friendship and responsibility go hand in hand.
  —John 15:1–17
- Extend friendship to those in need.—Galatians 6:1, 10

55. Frustration

- Where does a lot of frustration come from?
  —Ephesians 6:1–4

56. Gambling

- Wealth can bring on trouble.—Proverbs 15:16
- Wealth is temporal.—Proverbs 23:4–5
- Where are you looking for treasure?
  —Luke 12:15–34
- Balance greed with contentment.
  —1 Timothy 6:6–12

57. Gentleness

- Cultivate the spirit and attitude of a child of God.
  —2 Timothy 2:14–26
- Establishing peace starts with your tongue.
  —James 3:1–18

58. Gossip
    - Always speak the truth.—Exodus 23:1–9
    - Keep your tongue under control.—Psalm 34:13–14
    - Don't share everything you know.
      —Proverbs 11:11–13
    - Words can inflict injury.—Proverbs 25:18–28
    - Put out the fire of hot words.—Proverbs 26:20
    - Opening your mouth can be expensive.
      —Matthew 12:36
    - Don't dump your garbage on others.
      —Ephesians 4:29, 31
    - Do not be involved in gossip.
      —2 Thessalonians 3:6–15
    - Babbling on leads to ungodliness.
      —2 Timothy 2:16
    - You may have the thought, but lay it aside.
      —1 Peter 2:1

59. Greed
    - Learn to resist "King ME."—James 4:1–17

60. Guidance
    - Our Shepherd gently guides us.—Psalm 23:2–3
    - We can pray for His leading.—Psalm 23:2–3
    - God can clearly see the way.—Psalm 32:8
    - This fantastic promise has a condition.
      —Proverbs 3:5–6
    - We are being taught by the great Teacher.
      —John 14:26
    - God will guide us into all truth.—John 16:13

61. Guilt

- This joy and freedom can be yours.—Psalm 32:1–2
- There is no condemnation in Christ.
  —Romans 8:1–17
- Jesus took away our guilt.—2 Corinthians 5:21
- Great riches can be yours.—Ephesians 1:7
- Jesus has blotted out our guilt.
  —Colossians 2:9–17
- He washed us clean.—Titus 3:5–7
- God is greater than all of our guilt.—1 John 3:11–24

62. Habits

- The secret of breaking habits lies in abiding.
  —1 John 3:11–24

63. Happiness

- The word blessed means "happy."
  —Matthew 5:1–12
- Godliness is the source of contentment.
  —1 Timothy 6:3–10

64. Heaven

- Jesus is preparing a place for us.—John 14:1–14
- The focus of heaven changes our actions.
  —Colossians 3:1–17

65. Hell

- Watch your hot words.—Matthew 5:22
- There will be wailing and gnashing of teeth.
  —Matthew 13:42, 50
- Hell will be an everlasting fire.—Matthew 18:8–9

- Unbelievers will be cast into the outer darkness.
  —Matthew 22:13

- The fire of hell will never be extinguished.
  —Mark 9:48

- The promise of the judgment of God is ignored.
  —Romans 1:18–32

- This is the worst fire imaginable.—Romans 1:18–32

- There will be a lake of fire and brimstone.
  —Revelation 20:1–15

66. Help

- The idea of help is reinforced many times.
  —Psalm 46:1–11

- We not only receive help, but we give it to others.
  —Galatians 6:1–10

67. Homosexuality

- Do not have same-gender sex or sex with animals.
  —Leviticus 18:22–23

- God considers homosexuality an abomination.
  —Leviticus 20:13

- God gives rebellious people up to a life of disaster.
  —Romans 1:18–32

- Do not take this admonition casually.
  —1 Corinthians 6:9–11

- Crucify the old way of life.—Ephesians 4:22–24

- Do away with the old man and his actions.
  —Colossians 3:9–10

- Homosexuality is contrary to sound doctrine.
  —1 Timothy 1:1–11

- Victory over this sin is available.—Titus 3:5–6

68. Hope

- He will deliver your soul from death.
  —Psalm 33:18–22

- Hope and praise washes away despair.
  —Psalm 33:18–22

- God's care for you is guaranteed.—Psalm 121:1–8

- Through testing we glean patience and hope.
  —Romans 5:1–11

- God is the author of hope.—Romans 15:13

- God delivers above and beyond our wildest dreams.—Ephesians 3:20

- This is the hope of Christ's return.
  —1 Thessalonians 4:13–18

- We should live godly lives.—Titus 2:12–15

- Hope comes from a new life in Christ.—1 Peter 1:3

- Hope motivates and cleanses our life.
  —1 John 3:1–3

69. Hurt

- Jesus is the place to put your burdens.
  —Psalm 55:22

- Trust God when you are being tested.
  —Psalm 56:3–4

- Help comes when we focus toward heaven.
  —Psalm 121:1–8

- Cast all of your cares upon Him.—1 Peter 5:7

70. Immorality

- Our body is God's temple.—1 Corinthians 6:1–20

- Some do not heed the call for purity.
  —Revelation 9:13–21

71. Indecisiveness
   - You belong to Jesus—or you don't.
     —John 3:22–36

72. Inferiority
   - God is not inferior.—Psalm 63:3
   - God has the power over hell.—Psalm 86:13
   - God cared enough to form you in the womb.
     —Psalm 139:13–16
   - God uses what the world thinks is foolish.
     —1 Corinthians 1:26–31
   - We are chosen to praise God.—1 Peter 2:9–10

73. Insult
   - This is how the righteous should live.
     —Proverbs 12:1–28

74. Integrity
   - Learn the ways of God and the ways of living.
     —Psalm 25:1–22
   - God holds us accountable.—Luke 16:1–15

75. Jealousy
   - Jealousy rots the bones.—Proverbs 14:30
   - Do not envy those who get away with doing evil.
     —Proverbs 24:19–20
   - God will give rebellious people over to envy.
     —Romans 1:29
   - This is the lifestyle that makes a difference.
     —Romans 13:1–14
   - Love destroys envy.—1 Corinthians 13:4
   - Words of strife produce envy.—1 Timothy 6:4

- Envy is earthly, sensual, and devilish.
  —James 3:14–16

76. Joy

- Trusting in my Shield brings joy.—Psalm 28:7

- This joy that cannot be taken away.
  —John 16:20–22

- Being intoxicated with God brings joy.
  —Ephesians 5:18–19

- Gentleness, prayer, and thanksgiving cause joy.
  —Philippians 4:4–7

- Learn to look for joy in the middle of problems.
  —James 1:2–4

- Take on a new outlook toward difficulties.
  —1 Peter 4:12–13

77. Judging

- Take the beam out of your own eye.
  —Matthew 7:1–6

- How do I deal with the sin of fellow believers?
  —1 Corinthians 5:1–13

78. Kindness

- Learn to love your enemies.—Luke 6:27–36

- Put on the wardrobe of kindness and humility.
  —Colossians 3:1–17

79. Laziness

- If you don't work, you don't eat.
  —2 Thessalonians 3:6–15

- Be about God's business in the last days.
  —2 Peter 3:1–18

80. Lifestyle

- Jesus talks about a new way of behavior.
  —Matthew 5:1–12

- Run the race of life well.—1 Corinthians 9:1–27

- The path to becoming a faithful follower.
  —2 Timothy 2:14–26

81. Loneliness

- The Lord is always with you.—Joshua 1:9

- The Lord will provide all your needs—Psalm 23:1–6

- Others may disappoint, but God will not.
  —Psalm 27:10

- Someone is watching over you.—Psalm 91:11

- The Lord is your keeper.—Psalm 12:1–8

- God's right hand will uphold you.—Isaiah 41:10

- Deep waters will not overcome you.—Isaiah 43:1–3

- Where can you go to escape the Lord?
  —Matthew 28:20

- What do you think the word *never* means?
  —Hebrews 13:5–6

82. Lust

- Read advice from the oldest book in the Bible.
  —Job 31:1

- Jesus warns us about looking with lust.
  —Matthew 5:27–28

- Thoughts precede actions.—Mark 7:20–23

- Don't give up control of your life.—Romans 6:12

- We are in a constant battle.—Galatians 5:16–17

- Sex outside marriage is never right.
  —1 Thessalonians 4:3–8

- Run away from temptation!—2 Timothy 2:22

- You can tell the devil no.—James 1:13–15

83. Lying

- This is a quick way to get into trouble.
  —Proverbs 17:20

- Punishment is unavoidable.—Proverbs 19:9

- Covering wickedness is despised by everyone.
  —Proverbs 24:24

- Everyone around a liar follows his example.
  —Proverbs 29:12

- Flattery is a form of hatred.—Proverbs 26:28

- Just answer yes or no.—Matthew 5:37

- Learn to walk in honesty.—Ephesians 4:17–32

84. Materialism

- Which master do you serve?—Matthew 6:19–24

85. Morality

- God will look at how you have lived.—Romans 2:1–16

- Do not conform to the world.—Romans 12:1–8

86. Motives

- Who can begin to know the human heart?
  —Jeremiah 17:1–18

- Selfishness causes many problems.—James 4:1–12

87. Murder

- God's view of murder.—Numbers 35:6

- Money can cause people to murder.—James 5:1–6

88. Obedience

- Blessing comes from walking in God's ways.
—Deuteronomy 30:11–19

- Wisdom leads to understanding and obedience.
—Psalm 111:10

- Great rewards follow those who keep God's
word.—Psalm 119:2

- Judgment follows for all of our actions.
—Ecclesiastes 12:13–14

- Willingness and obedience have a reward.
—Isaiah 1:16–20

- Everyone serves someone.—Matthew 6:24

- Love is the key to obedience.—John 14:15, 21

- The obedience of one Man changed everything.
—Romans 5:1–21

- Which way are you going to yield?—Romans 6:16

- Bring your thoughts into captivity.
—2 Corinthians 10:5

- Keeping the whole Law is impossible.—James 2:10

- Obedience affects our prayers.—1 John 3:22

89. Occult

- God condemns wizards.—Leviticus 20:27

- Playing with the spirits is an abomination.
—Deuteronomy 18:9–13

- Saul calls on the witch of Endor.
—1 Samuel 28:7–12

- Avoid dabbling in spiritism.—2 Kings 21:6

- Consulting wizards is wrong.—Isaiah 8:19

- God destroys the charmers.—Isaiah 19:3

- Avoid astrology and fortunetellers.
  —Isaiah 47:13–14

- Burn the magic books.—Acts 19:18–20

- Run from anything to do with the occult.
  —James 4:7

90. Overcoming Temptation

- God will hold on to your hand.—Isaiah 41:10

- Pray to overcome temptation.—Matthew 26:41

- All temptation is common.—1 Corinthians 10:13

- God will change you for the better.—Philippians 1:6

- God promises to help keep us from evil.
  —2 Thessalonians 3:3

- There is a part we play.—James 4:7

- God called us out of darkness.—1 Peter 2:9

91. Pain

- Follow Christ's example when in pain.
  —Hebrews 12:1–13

92. Patience

- Waiting develops strength of character.
  —Isaiah 40:31

- Patience produces contentment.—Philippians 4:11

- The exercise of faith builds patience.—James 1:2–4

- Patience glitters like gold.—2 Peter 1:5–8

93. Peace

- God lifts us up when we are down.—Psalm 3:1–8

- Focusing on God produces peace.—Isaiah 26:3–4

- There is great peace ahead.—John 14:1–31

- The victory of Christ produces peace. — John 16:33
- Make peace with God. — Romans 5:1–11
- Here is the secret for finding peace.
  — Philippians 4:4–9
- Let God's peace reign. — Colossians 3:15

94. Pornography

- Guard the eyes from sinfulness. — Job 31:1
- Keep your thought life pure. — Psalm 119:9–11
- Do not let your thoughts stray. — Matthew 5:27–28
- Put to death [mortify] sensual thoughts.
  — Colossians 3:5
- Here is God's will about sex.
  — 1 Thessalonians 4:3–8

95. Premarital Sex

- Does premarital sex glorify God?
  — 1 Corinthians 6:18–20
- Marital sex is God ordained. — 1 Corinthians 7:2, 9, 36
- This is straight talk about premarital sex.
  — 1 Thessalonians 4:3–8

96. Priorities

- Choose the right path to follow. — Proverbs 3:1–35
- Seek after God's righteousness. — Matthew 6:25–34

97. Problems

- Develop a positive outlook toward difficulties.
  — James 1:1–18

98. Procrastination

- Hard work makes the sluggard's teeth hurt.
  — Proverbs 10:1–32

- Talk produces very little; labor stands the test.
  —Proverbs 14:23

- The worth of the objective determines the effort.
  —Proverbs 26:1–28

- The foolish girls did not plan ahead.
  —Matthew 25:2–13

- Find the best use of your time.
  —Ephesians 5:15–17

- Learn to be earnest and disciplined.—1 Peter 4:7

99. Quarrels

- Keep your mouth in control and save your life.
  —Proverbs 13:1–10

- Learn to stay away from foolish arguments.
  —Titus 3:1–11

- Discover the source of fighting and war.
  —James 4:1–12

100. Rebellion

- God sees rebellion and witchcraft as the same
  sin.—1 Samuel 15:22–29

- The rebellious hate reproof.—Proverbs 12:1

- Poverty and shame follow rebellion.
  —Proverbs 13:13, 18

- Destruction can be the result of rebellion.
  —Proverbs 29:1

- The law exposes the rebellious.—1 Timothy 1:8–10

101. Relationships

- Use this standard for evaluating relationships.
  —2 Corinthians 6:14–18

- Start a new relationship with God.
  —Ephesians 2:11–22

102. Resentment

- Resentment comes from a lack of trust.
  —James 1:1–27

103. Revenge

- Get the ultimate revenge—do good to others.
  —Romans 12:17–21

104. Righteousness

- How can I have a clean heart?—Psalm 51:1–19

- Do away with the old man and bring on the new.
  —2 Corinthians 5:11–21

105. Self-Centeredness

- Man's way is not God's way.—Mark 8:31–38

- Turn your focus from self to others.
  —1 Peter 1:14–25

106. Self-Image

- God looks at your heart and your motivation.
  —1 Samuel 16:7

- God formed us and determines each of our days.
  —Psalm 139:13–16

- We must face our own conceits.—Romans 12:10, 16

- God cared so much that He chose us.
  —Ephesians 1:3–6, 11–14

- God will work out His plan in our lives.
  —Philippians 1:6

- Care about each other.—Philippians 2:3–4

107. Selfishness

- The know-it-all is selfish. —Mark 8:31–38
- Two unselfish people never get a divorce. —Mark 10:4
- Become interested in others. —Romans 15:2–3
- Seek to put others ahead of yourself. —1 Corinthians 10:24
- Shy away from your own glory. —Philippians 2:3–4
- Selfishness causes wars, adultery, and helps Satan. —James 4:1–10

108. Sexual Immorality

- Seek happiness with your own wife. —Proverbs 5:15–21
- This is the Bible's example of a love affair. —Song of Solomon 1–8
- The Bible has a plan for everyone. —1 Corinthians 7:1–11
- Here is training for husbands and wives. —Ephesians 5:18–6:3
- Extramarital sex is sin. —1 Thessalonians 4:1–8
- The marriage bed is undefiled. —Hebrews 13:4
- Here is a husband/wife training manual. —1 Peter 3:1–9

109. Sexual Purity

- It is better to marry than burn with lust. —1 Corinthians 7:36–37
- Fornication is forbidden. —Ephesians 5:3
- Abstain from all sexual immorality. —Colossians 3:5

- God wants us to remain sexually pure.
  —1 Thessalonians 4:3–7

- God will judge sexual sin.—Hebrews 13:4

110. Sickness

- God will be with you in times of trouble.
  —Psalm 41:3

- It is God who heals diseases.—Psalm 103:3

- Jesus was touched by the sickness of mankind.
  —Matthew 4:23

- God can take sickness and turn it into His glory.
  —John 11:4

- Encourage others to join you in prayer.
  —James 5:13–15

111. Sin

- We have gone our own way.—Isaiah 53:5–6

- A great chasm stretches between man and God.
  —Isaiah 59:1–2

- Sin will enslave a person.—John 8:34

- Everyone has sinned.—Romans 3:23

- Sin pays a poor wage.—Romans 6:23

- God is not fooled by our behavior.—Galatians 6:7–8

112. Spiritual Warfare

- Jesus faced temptations in the wilderness.
  —Matthew 4:1–11

- This suit of armor is for fighting spiritual battles.
  —Ephesians 6:10–18

- The devil is defeated.—James 4:7

- God is greater than the devil or any of his attacks.
  —1 John 4:4

113. Stealing

- God forbids stealing.—Exodus 20:15
- Riches can steal your heart away.—Psalm 62:10
- Give me neither poverty nor riches.
  —Proverbs 30:7–9
- If you have stolen—repent and stop.
  —Ephesians 4:28

114. Stress

- Worry only produces more worry.—Matthew 6:27, 33–34
- Trouble can make you grow and mature.
  —Romans 5:1–5
- When under stress change your thinking pattern.
  —Philippians 4:4–9
- Cast your anxieties on Jesus.—1 Peter 5:7

115. Suffering

- Present suffering will bring future rewards.
  —Romans 8:18
- As sufferings increase so does Christ's consolation.—2 Corinthians 1:5
- We will suffer for the cause of Christ.
  —Philippians 1:29
- Join in Christ's sufferings.—Philippians 3:10
- We will one day reign with Him.—2 Timothy 2:12
- Suffering develops strength of character.
  —James 1:2–8
- Your suffering will one day bring glory.
  —1 Peter 1:6–7

- Suffering can result from your own wrongdoing.
  —1 Peter 2:19

- Suffering for Christ will be rewarded.
  —1 Peter 4:12–13, 16

- Suffering can mellow us if we learn from it.
  —1 Peter 5:10

116. Suicidal Thoughts

- Every man has a day of death.—Job 14:5

- When in trouble, call on God to help.
  —Psalm 50:15

- Complain to God when your spirit is overwhelmed.
  —Psalm 77:7–15

- God is your refuge.—Psalm 91:1–2

- God will hear you call and will answer.
  —Jeremiah 33:3

- Learn to quietly wait.—Lamentations 3:22–24

- God is your stronghold during trouble.—Nahum 1:7

- Do you need rest?—Matthew 11:28

- Abundant life can be yours.—John 10:10

- We are connected with others.—Romans 14:7

- Your body belongs to God.—1 Corinthians 6:19–20

- Overcome the temptation to commit suicide.
  —James 4:7

- Be alert to your enemy.—1 Peter 5:8–10

117. Temptation

- Slippery feet need a firm foundation.
  —Psalm 94:17–18

- Forsake your sins and prosper.—Psalm 94:17–18

- Watch and pray to overcome temptation.
  —Matthew 26:41

- God will provide a way of escape.
  —1 Corinthians 10:12–13

- Jesus was tempted—He can help you.
  —Hebrews 2:18

- We have a High Priest who helps us.
  —Hebrews 4:14–16

- Sometimes we bring on our own problems.
  —James 1:2–14

- Resist the devil.—James 4:7

- Get the right attitude.—1 Peter 1:6

- The Lord will deliver the godly.—2 Peter 2:9

- A greater power lives within you.—1 John 4:4

- There is Someone who can keep you from falling.
  —Jude 1:24

118. Terminal Illness

- God knows your thoughts during this struggle.
  —Jeremiah 29:11–13

- Sometimes there is healing.—2 Corinthians 12:9

- Learn to give thanks in everything.
  —1 Thessalonians 5:18

119. Thankfulness

- It is a good thing to give thanks.—Psalm 92:1–15

- Here are the results of not being thankful.
  —Romans 1:18–23

- Be grateful for your salvation.—Ephesians 2:1–10

120. Trials

- Trials bring results. —Job 23:10

- Trials produce endurance and godliness.
  —Romans 5:3–5

- Our trials can be used to help others.
  —2 Corinthians 1:3–5

- Our weakness demonstrates God's greatness.
  —2 Corinthians 12:7–10

- Trials produce patience. —James 1:2–5, 12

- Trials test our character. —1 Peter 1:6–7

- Trials help us appreciate what Christ did for us.
  —1 Peter 4:12–13

121. Unpardonable Sin

- Do not speak against the Holy Spirit.
  —Matthew 12:22–32

- Do not blaspheme the Holy Spirit. —Mark 3:22–30

- Blasphemy against the Holy Spirit is unforgivable.
  —Luke 12:10

- What is a sin unto death? —1 John 5:16–17

122. Waiting

- Be of good courage and strengthen your heart.
  —Psalm 27:1–14

- Escape from the horrible pit and the miry clay.
  —Psalm 40:1–4

- Wait for Christ's return. —Matthew 24:32–51

123. Weakness

- God's strength is made perfect in weakness.
  —2 Corinthians 12:1–10

- Weakness is caused by sin.—1 John 3:1–11

124. Will of God

- Rest and wait patiently.—Psalm 46:10

- Claim God as your refuge.—Psalm 91:1–2

- God will direct your paths.—Proverbs 3:5–6

- Examine your own work.—Galatians 6:4

- Awaken to His will for your life.
  —Ephesians 5:14–21

- Work out your own salvation.—Philippians 2:12–13

- Stay sexually pure.—1 Thessalonians 4:3

- Give thanks in everything.—1 Thessalonians 5:18

- Be willing to suffer for Christ.—1 Peter 3:17

125. Worry

- Do not fear or be dismayed.—Isaiah 41:10, 13

- Do not worry about food, drink, or clothing.
  —Matthew 6:25–34

- Do not forget to be thankful.—Philippians 4:6–9, 19

- Do not forget that God will never leave you.
  —Hebrews 13:5–6

- Don't forget to cast your cares on God.
  —1 Peter 5:6–7

■LIST #49
365 Days to Read through the Bible

Here's an easy plan to help you read through the whole
Bible in one year.

January

1   Genesis 1–2

2   Genesis 3–5

3   Genesis 6–9

4   Genesis 10–11

5   Genesis 12–15

6   Genesis 16–19

7   Genesis 20–22

8   Genesis 23–26

9   Genesis 27–29

10 Genesis 30–32

11 Genesis 33–36

12 Genesis 37–39

13 Genesis 40–42

14 Genesis 43–46

15 Genesis 47–50

16 Job 1–4

17 Job 5–7

18 Job 8–10

19 Job 11–13

20 Job 14–17

21 Job 18–20

22 Job 21–24

23 Job 25–27

24 Job 28–31

25 Job 32–34

26 Job 35–37

27 Job 38–42

28 Exodus 1–4

29 Exodus 5–7

30 Exodus 8–10

31 Exodus 11–13

February

1 Exodus 14–17

2 Exodus 18–20

3 Exodus 21–24

4 Exodus 25–27

5 Exodus 28–31

6 Exodus 32–34

 7   Exodus 35–37

 8   Exodus 38–40

 9   Leviticus 1–4

10   Leviticus 5–7

11   Leviticus 8–10

12   Leviticus 11–13

13   Leviticus 14–16

14   Leviticus 17–19

15   Leviticus 20–23

16   Leviticus 24–27

17   Numbers 1–3

18   Numbers 4–6

19   Numbers 7–10

20   Numbers 11–14

21   Numbers 15–17

22   Numbers 18–20

23   Numbers 21–24

24   Numbers 25–27

25   Numbers 28–30

26   Numbers 31–33

27   Numbers 34–36

28   Deuteronomy 1–3

March

23 Judges 16–18

24 Judges 19–21

25 Ruth 1–4

26 1 Samuel 1–3

27 1 Samuel 4–7

28 1 Samuel 8–10

29 1 Samuel 11–13

30 1 Samuel 14–16

31 1 Samuel 17–20

April

1 1 Samuel 21–24

2 1 Samuel 25–28

3 1 Samuel 29–31

4 2 Samuel 1–4

5 2 Samuel 5–8

6 2 Samuel 9–12

7 2 Samuel 13–15

8 2 Samuel 16–18

9 2 Samuel 19–21

10 2 Samuel 22–24

11 Psalms 1–3

12 Psalms 4–6

13 Psalms 7–9

14 Psalms 10–12

15 Psalms 13–15

16 Psalms 16–18

17 Psalms 19–21

18 Psalms 22–24

19 Psalms 25–27

20 Psalms 28–30

21 Psalms 31–33

22 Psalms 34–36

23 Psalms 37–39

24 Psalms 40–42

25 Psalms 43–45

26 Psalms 46–48

27 Psalms 49–51

28 Psalms 52–54

29 Psalms 55–57

30 Psalms 58–60

May

1 Psalms 61–63

2 Psalms 64–66

3 Psalms 67–69

4 Psalms 70–72

 5 Psalms 73–75

 6 Psalms 76–78

 7 Psalms 79–81

 8 Psalms 82–84

 9 Psalms 85–87

10 Psalms 88–90

11 Psalms 91–93

12 Psalms 94–96

13 Psalms 97–99

14 Psalms 100–102

15 Psalms 103–105

16 Psalms 106–108

17 Psalms 109–111

18 Psalms 112–114

19 Psalms 115–118

20 Psalm 119

21 Psalms 120–123

22 Psalms 124–126

23 Psalms 127–129

24 Psalms 130–132

25 Psalms 133–135

26 Psalms 136–138

June

17   1 Kings 8–10

18   1 Kings 11–13

19   1 Kings 14–16

20   1 Kings 17–19

21   I Kings 20–22

22   2 Kings 1–3

23   2 Kings 4–6

24   2 Kings 7–10

25   2 Kings 11–14:20

26   Joel 1–3

27   2 Kings 14:21–25; Jonah 1–4

28   2 Kings 14:26–29; Amos 1–3

29   Amos 4–6

30   Amos 7–9

July

1   2 Kings 15–17

2   Hosea 1–4

3   Hosea 5–7

4   Hosea 8–10

5   Hosea 11–14

6   2 Kings 18–19

7   Isaiah 1–3

31 Nahum 1–3

August

1 2 Kings 20–21

2 Zephaniah 1–3

3 Habakkuk 1–3

4 2 Kings 22–25

5 Obadiah; Jeremiah 1–2

6 Jeremiah 3–5

7 Jeremiah 6–8

8 Jeremiah 9–12

9 Jeremiah 13–16

10 Jeremiah 17–20

11 Jeremiah 21–23

12 Jeremiah 24–26

13 Jeremiah 27–29

14 Jeremiah 30–32

15 Jeremiah 33–36

16 Jeremiah 37–39

17 Jeremiah 40–42

18 Jeremiah 43–46

19 Jeremiah 47–49

20 Jeremiah 50–52

12   Ezekiel 4–7

13   Ezekiel 8–11

14   Ezekiel 12–14

15   Ezekiel 15–18

16   Ezekiel 19–21

17   Ezekiel 22–24

18   Ezekiel 25–27

19   Ezekiel 28–30

20   Ezekiel 31–33

21   Ezekiel 34–36

22   Ezekiel 37–39

23   Ezekiel 40–42

24   Ezekiel 43–45

25   Ezekiel 46–48

26   Daniel 1–3

27   Daniel 4–6

28   Daniel 7–9

29   Daniel 10–12

30   Esther 1–3

October

1   Esther 4–7

2   Esther 8–10

3   Ezra 1–4

4 Haggai 1–2; Zechariah 1–2

5 Zechariah 3–6

6 Zechariah 7–10

7 Zechariah 11–14

8 Ezra 5–7

9 Ezra 8–10

10 Nehemiah 1–3

11 Nehemiah 4–6

12 Nehemiah 7–9

13 Nehemiah 10–13

14 Malachi 1–4

15 Matthew 1–4

16 Matthew 5–7

17 Matthew 8–11

18 Matthew 12–15

19 Matthew 16–19

20 Matthew 20–22

21 Matthew 23–25

22 Matthew 26–28

23 Mark 1–3

24 Mark 4–6

25 Mark 7–10

26 Mark 11–13

27 Mark 14–16

28 Luke 1–3

29 Luke 4–6

30 Luke 7–9

31 Luke 10–13

November

1 Luke 14–17

2 Luke 18–21

3 Luke 22–24

4 John 1–3

5 John 4–6

6 John 7–10

7 John 11–13

8 John 14–17

9 John 18–21

10 Acts 1–2

11 Acts 3–5

12 Acts 6–9

13 Acts 10–12

14 Acts 13–14

15 James 1–2

16 James 3–5

17 Galatians 1–3

18 Galatians 4–6

19 Acts 15–18:11

20 1 Thessalonians 1–5

21 2 Thessalonians 1–3; Acts 18:12–19:10

22 1 Corinthians 1–4

23 1 Corinthians 5–8

24 1 Corinthians 9–12

25 1 Corinthians 13–16

26 Acts 19:11–20:1; 2 Corinthians 1–3

27 2 Corinthians 4–6

28 2 Corinthians 7–9

29 2 Corinthians 10–13

30 Acts 20:2; Romans 1–4

December

1 Romans 5–8

2 Romans 9–11

3 Romans 12–16

4 Acts 20:3–22:30

5 Acts 23–25

6 Acts 26–28

7 Ephesians 1–3

8 Ephesians 4–6

9   Philippians 1–4

10   Colossians 1–4

11   Hebrews 1–4

12   Hebrews 5–7

13   Hebrews 8–10

14   Hebrews 11–13

15   Philemon; 1 Peter 1–2

16   1 Peter 3–5

17   2 Peter 1–3

18   1 Timothy 1–3

19   1 Timothy 4–6

20   2 Timothy

21   Titus 1–3

22   1 John 1–2

23   1 John 3–5

24   2 John; 3 John; Jude

25   Revelation 1–3

26   Revelation 4–6

27   Revelation 7–9

28   Revelation 10–12

29   Revelation 13–15

30   Revelation 16–18

31   Revelation 19–22

LIST #50
189 Heavenly Quotations

This collection of quotes from throughout history will inspire and encourage you.

Agnosticism

1. An agnostic found himself in trouble, and a friend suggested he pray. "How can I pray when I do not know whether or not there is a God?" he asked. "If you are lost in the forest," his friend replied, "you do not wait until you find someone before shouting for help."—Dan Plies

Atheism

2. To be an atheist requires an infinitely greater measure of faith than to receive all the great truths which atheism would deny.—Joseph Addison

3. I can see how it might be possible for a man to look down upon the earth and be an atheist, but I cannot conceive how he could look up into the heavens and say there is no God.—Abraham Lincoln

4. The three great apostles of practical atheism that make converts without persecuting, and retain them without preaching, are health, wealth, and power.—Charles Caleb Colton

5. An atheist is a man who has no invisible means of support.—John Buchan

Bible

6. The best evidence that the Bible is the inspired word of God is to be found within its covers. It proves itself.—Charles Hodge

7. I have made it a practice for several years to read the Bible in the course of every year.—John Quincy Adams

8. All that I am I owe to Jesus Christ, revealed to me in His divine Book.—David Livingstone

9. The New Testament is the best book the world has ever known or will know.—Charles Dickens

10. For more than a thousand years the Bible, collectively taken, has gone hand in hand with civilization, science, law—in short, with the moral and intellectual cultivation of the species, always supporting and often leading the way.—Samuel Taylor Coleridge

11. The book to read is not the one which thinks for you, but the one which makes you think. No book in the world equals the Bible for that.—James McCosh

12. No man ever did, or ever will become most truly eloquent without being a constant reader of the Bible, and admirer of the purity and sublimity of its language.—Fisher Ames

13. It was the Lord who put into my mind (I could feel His hand upon me) the fact that it would be possible to sail from here to the Indies. All who heard of my project rejected it with laughter, ridiculing me. There is no question that the inspiration was from the Holy Spirit, because He comforted me with rays of marvelous inspiration from the Holy Scriptures.
   —Christopher Columbus

14. When you have read the Bible, you will know it is the word of God, because you will have found it the key to your own heart, your own happiness and your own duty.—Woodrow Wilson

15. It is impossible to mentally or socially enslave a Bible-reading people.—Horace Greeley

16. Hold fast to the Bible as the sheet-anchor of your liberties; write its precepts in your hearts and practice them in your lives. To the influence of this book we are indebted for all the progress made in true civilization, and to this we must look as our guide for the future.—Ulysses S. Grant

17. Defend the Bible? I would just as soon defend a lion. Just turn the Bible loose. It will defend itself.
—Charles Haddon Spurgeon

18. The Bible is one of the greatest blessings bestowed by God on the children of men. It has God for its author; salvation for its end, and truth without any mixture for its matter. It is all pure, all sincere; nothing too much; nothing wanting.—John Locke

19. I have always said . . . that the studious perusal of the sacred volume will make better citizens, better fathers, and better husbands.—Thomas Jefferson

20. This great book is the best gift God has given to man. . . . But for it we could not know right from wrong.
—Abraham Lincoln

21. Read Demosthenes or Cicero; read Plato, Aristotle, or any others of that class; I grant you that you will be attracted, delighted, moved, enraptured by them in a surprising manner; but if, after reading them, you turn to the perusal of the sacred volume, whether you are willing or unwilling, it will affect you so power-

fully, it will so penetrate your heart, and impress itself so strangely on your mind that, compared with its energetic influence, the beauties of rhetoricians and philosophers will almost entirely disappear; so that it is easy to perceive something divine in the sacred Scriptures, which far surpasses the highest attainments and ornaments of human industry.
—John Calvin

22. The Bible is worth all other books that have ever been printed.—Patrick Henry

23. So great is my veneration for the Bible, that the earlier my children begin to read it the more confident will be my hopes that they will prove useful citizens to their country and respectable members of society.
—John Quincy Adams

24. I speak as a man of the world to men of the world; and I say to you, Search the Scriptures! The Bible is the book of all others, to be read at all ages, and in all conditions of human life; not to be read once or twice or thrice through, and then laid aside, but to be read in small portions of one or two chapters every day, and never to be intermitted, unless by some overruling necessity.—John Quincy Adams

25. Most people are bothered by those passages in Scripture which they cannot understand; but as for me, I always notice that the passages in Scripture which trouble me most are those which I do understand.—Mark Twain

26. The Bible is God's chart for you to steer by, to keep you from the bottom of the sea, and to show you where the harbor is, and how to reach it without running on rocks or bars.—Henry Ward Beecher

27. The Bible was never intended to be a book for scholars and specialists only. From the very beginning it was intended to be everybody's book, and that is what it continues to be.—F. F. Bruce

28. The Bible is a window in this prison-world, through which we may look into eternity.—Timothy Dwight

29. Nobody ever outgrows Scripture, the book widens and deepens with our years.—Charles Haddon Spurgeon

30. It is not possible to ever exhaust the mind of the Scriptures. It is a well that has no bottom. —John Chrysostom

31. I would advise no one to send his child where the Holy Scriptures are not supreme. Every institution that does not unceasingly pursue the study of God's word becomes corrupt.—Martin Luther

Christ

32. The great mistake of my life has been that I tried to be moral without faith in Jesus; but I have learned that true morality can only keep pace with trust in Christ as my Savior.—Gerrit Smith

33. If Socrates would enter the room we should rise and do him honor. But if Jesus Christ came into the room we should fall down on our knees and worship Him. —Napoleon Bonaparte

34. I search in vain in history to find the similar to Jesus Christ, or anything which can approach the gospel. Neither history, nor humanity, nor the ages, nor nature, offer me anything with which I am able to compare or explain it. There is nothing there which is not beyond the march of events and above the human

mind. What happiness it gives to those who believe it! What marvels there which those admire who reflect upon it!—Napoleon Bonaparte

35. As the print of the seal on the wax is the express image of the seal itself, so Christ is the express image—the perfect representation of God.—Ambrose of Milan

36. In his life, Christ is an example, showing us how to live; in his death, he is a sacrifice, satisfying for our sins; in his resurrection, a conqueror; in his ascension, a king; in his intercession, a high priest.
—Martin Luther

37. Alexander, Caesar, Charlemagne, and I myself have founded great empires. . . . But Jesus alone founded His empire upon love, and to this very day, millions would die for Him. Jesus Christ was more than a man.—Napoleon Bonaparte

38. The sum of the whole matter is this, that our civilization cannot survive materially unless it be redeemed spiritually. It can be saved only by becoming permeated with the spirit of Christ and being made free and happy by the practices which spring out of that spirit.
—Woodrow Wilson

39. To be like Christ is to be a Christian.—William Penn

40. There is no greater drama in human record than the sight of a few Christians, scorned or oppressed by a succession of emperors, bearing all trials with a fierce tenacity, multiplying quietly, building order while their enemies generated chaos, fighting the sword with the word, brutality with hope, and at last defeating the strongest state that history has known. Caesar and Christ had met in the arena, and Christ had won.
—Will Durant

41. The sages and heroes of history are receding from us. But time has no power over the name and deeds and words of Jesus Christ.—William Ellery Channing

42. Philosophical argument, especially that drawn from the vastness of the universe, in comparison with the apparent insignificance of this globe, has sometimes shaken my reason for the faith which is in me; but my heart has always assured me that the gospel of Jesus Christ must be divine reality. The Sermon on the Mount cannot be a mere human production. This belief enters into the very depth of my conscience. The whole history of man proves it.—Daniel Webster

Christianity

43. There is one single fact which we may oppose to all the wit and argument of infidelity, namely, that no man ever repented of being a Christian on his death-bed. —Hannah More

44. Going to church doesn't make you a Christian any more than going to a garage makes you an automobile. —William Ashley (Billy) Sunday

45. There never was found in any age of the world either philosopher or sect, or law, or discipline which did so highly exalt the public good as the Christian faith. —Francis Bacon

46. Whatever makes men good Christians makes them good citizens.—Daniel Webster

47. Christianity has not been tried and found wanting; it has been found difficult and not tried. —G. K. Chesterton

48. Christianity everywhere gives dignity to labor, sanctity to marriage, and brotherhood to man. Where it may

not convince, it enlightens; where it does not convert it restrains; where it does not renew, it refines; where it does not sanctify, it subdues and elevates. It is profitable alike for this world, and for the world that is to come.—Sir George St. Patrick Lawrence

49. When a man is opposed to Christianity, it is because Christianity is opposed to him. Your infidel is usually a person who resents the opposition of Christianity to that in his nature and life which Jesus came to rebuke and destroy.—Robert Hall

50. Whatever men may think of religion, the historic fact is, that in proportion as the institutions of Christianity lose their hold upon the multitudes, the fabric of society is in peril.—Arthur Tappan Pierson

51. Christianity is the companion of liberty in all its conflicts, the cradle of its infancy, and the divine source of its claims.—Alexis de Tocqueville

52. The distinction between Christianity and all other systems of religion consists largely in this, that in these others men are found seeking after God, while Christianity is God seeking after men.
—Thomas Arnold

53. Where science speaks of improvement, Christianity speaks of renovation; where science speaks of development, Christianity speaks of sanctification; where science speaks of progress, Christianity speaks of perfection.—Joseph Parrish Thompson

54. The real security of Christianity is to be found in its benevolent morality; in its exquisite adaptation to the human heart; in the facility with which it accommodates itself to the capacity of every human intellect; in the consolation which it bears to every house of

mourning; and in the light with which it brightens
the great mystery of the grave.—Thomas Babington
Macaulay

Church

55. The church is looking for better methods; God is
looking for better men.—E. M. Bounds

Creator

56. All I have seen teaches me to trust the Creator for all I
have not seen.—Ralph Waldo Emerson

Devil

57. The devil is an optimist if he thinks he can make
people meaner.—Karl Kraus

58. Let the devil get into the church, and he will mount
the altar.—Author Unknown

59. It is easy to bid the devil be your guest, but difficult
to get rid of him.—Author Unknown

60. Better keep the devil at the door than turn him out of
the house.—Author Unknown

61. He that is embarked with the devil must sail with
him.—Author Unknown

62. The devil can quote Scripture.—Author Unknown

Discipleship

63. Salvation is free, but discipleship costs us everything
we have.—Billy Graham

64. No horse gets anywhere until he is harnessed. No
steam or gas ever drives anything until it is confined.
No Niagara is ever turned into light and power until

it is tunneled. No life ever grows great until it is focused, dedicated, disciplined.—Harry Emerson Fosdick

Evangelism

65. Evangelism is not a professional job for a few trained men, but is instead the unrelenting responsibility of every person who belongs, even in the most modest way, to the company of Jesus.—Elton Trueblood

Faith

66. Faith is a gift of God.—Blaise Pascal

67. Faith is the divine evidence whereby the spiritual man discerneth God, and the things of God.
    —John Wesley

68. The primary cause of unhappiness in the world today is . . . lack of faith.—Carl Jung

69. Faith is like radar that sees through the fog—the reality of things at a distance that the human eye cannot see.—Corrie Ten Boom

70. Pity the human being who is not able to connect faith within himself with the infinite. . . . He who has faith has . . . an inward reservoir of courage, hope, confidence, calmness, and assuring trust that all will come out well—even though to the world it may appear to come out most badly.—B. C. Forbes

71. Granted that faith cannot be proved, what harm will come to you if you gamble on its truth and it proves false? . . . If you gain, you gain all; if you lose, you lose nothing. —Blaise Pascal

72. This is the art of courage: to see things as they are and

still believe that the victory lies not with those who avoid the bad, but those who taste, in living awareness, every drop of the good.—Victoria Lincoln

73. Faith makes the uplook good, the outlook bright, the inlook favorable, and the future glorious.
—V. Raymond Edman

74. Skepticism has never founded empires, established principles, or changed the world's heart. The great doers in history have always been men of faith.
—Edwin Hubbel Chapin

75. Any featherhead can have confidence in times of victory, but the test is to have faith when things are going wrong. —Winston Churchill

76. I admire the serene assurance of those who have religious faith. It is wonderful to observe the calm confidence of a Christian with four aces. —Mark Twain

77. Faith is a Fantastic Adventure In Trusting Him.
—Corrie ten Boom

78. God hasn't called me to be successful. He's called me to be faithful.—Mother Teresa

79. There is one inevitable criterion of judgment touching religious faith in doctrinal matters. Can you reduce it to practice? If not, have none of it.—Hosea Ballou

80. Faith is an outward and visible sign of an inward and spiritual grace.—Author Unknown

81. The great act of faith is when man decides that he is not God.—Oliver Wendell Holmes

Forgiveness

82. I firmly believe a great many prayers are not answered because we are not willing to forgive someone.—Dwight L. Moody

83. If the other person injures you, you may forget the injury; but if you injure him you will always remember.
—Kahlil Gribran

84. It is easier to forgive an enemy than a friend.
—Madame Dorothee Deluzy

85. One of the secrets of a long and fruitful life is to forgive everybody everything every night before you go to bed.—Author Unknown

86. If thou wouldst find much favor and peace with God and man, be very low in thine own eyes. Forgive thyself little and others much.—Robert Leighton

87. We can forgive almost anything except the person who has to forgive us.—Author Unknown

88. To understand is to forgive.—French Proverb

89. He that cannot forgive others breaks the bridge over which he must pass himself; for every man has need to be forgiven.—Thomas Fuller

90. Forgiveness is the oil of relationships.
—Josh McDowell

91. Forgiveness means letting go of the past.
—Gerald Jampolsky

92. Forgiveness is not an elective in the curriculum of life. It is a required course, and the exams are always tough to pass.—Charles Swindoll

93. The remedy for wrongs is to forget them.
—Publilius Syrus

94. The more a man knows the more he forgives.
—Catherine the Great

95. Forgiveness needs to be accepted, as well as offered, before it is complete.—C. S. Lewis

96. A Christian will find it cheaper to pardon than to resent. Forgiveness saves the expense of anger, the cost of hatred, the waste of spirits.
—Hannah More

97. If men wound you with injuries, meet them with patience: hasty words rankle the wound, soft language dresses it, forgiveness cures it, and oblivion takes away the scar. It is more noble by silence to avoid an injury than by argument to overcome it.
—Francis Beaumont

98. The weak can never forgive. Forgiveness is the attribute of the strong.—Gandhi

99. Forgiveness is the fragrance the violet sheds on the heel that has crushed it.—Mark Twain

100. Sometimes we find it hard to forgive. We forget that forgiveness is as much for us as for the other person. If you can't forgive it's like holding a hot coal in your hand—you're the one getting burned. The tension may be hurting you much more than the other person.—Jennifer James

101. Doing an injury puts you below your enemy; revenging one makes you but even with him; forgiving it sets you above him.—Benjamin Franklin

102. Forgiveness is not a feeling but a promise or commitment to the following three things:
    1. I will not use it against them in the future.
    2. I will not talk to others about them.
    3. I will not dwell on it my self.—Jay E. Adams

God

103. God is not a cosmic bell-boy for whom we can press a button to get things.—Harry Emerson Fosdick

104. Two men please God—who serves Him with all his heart because he knows Him; who seeks Him with all his heart because he knows Him not.—Nikita Ivanovich Panin

105. Disregard the study of God and you sentence yourself to stumble and blunder throughout life, blindfolded, as it were, with no sense of direction and no understanding of what surrounds you.—James I. Packer

106. It is only from the belief of the goodness and wisdom of a supreme being, that our calamities can be borne in the manner which becomes a man.—Henry Mackenzie

107. In what way, or by what manner of working God changes a soul from evil to good—how he impregnates the barren rock with priceless gems and gold—is, to the human mind, an impenetrable mystery. —Samuel Taylor Coleridge

108. We have been the recipients of the choicest bounties of heaven; we have been preserved these many years in peace and prosperity; we have grown in number, wealth, and power as no other nation has ever grown. But we have forgotten God! Intoxicated with unbroken success, we have become too self-sufficient to feel the necessity of redeeming and preserving grace, too proud to pray to the God who made us.—Abraham Lincoln

109. Belief in and dependence on God is absolutely essential. It will be an integral part of our public life as long as I am Governor.—Ronald Reagan

110. Of all kinds of knowledge that we can ever obtain, the knowledge of God and the knowledge of ourselves are the most important.—Jonathan Edwards

111. Sometimes a nation abolishes God, but fortunately God is more tolerant.—Herbert V. Prochnow

112. If we spend sixteen hours a day dealing with tangible things and only five minutes a day dealing with God, is it any wonder that tangible things are two hundred times more real to us than God?—William R. Inge

113. The God who gave us life, gave us liberty at the same time.—Thomas Jefferson

114. Often God has to shut a door in our face so that He can subsequently open the door through which He wants us to go.—Catherine Marshall

115. I know that the Lord is always on the side of the right. But it is my constant anxiety and prayer that I and this nation should be on the Lord's side. —Abraham Lincoln

116. No people can be bound to acknowledge and adore the Invisible Hand which conducts the affairs of men more than those of the United States. —George Washington

117. Government laws are needed to give us civil rights, and God is needed to make us civil. —Reverend Ralph W. Sockman

118. A man can no more diminish God's glory by refusing to worship him than a lunatic can put out the sun by scribbling the word "darkness" on the walls of his cell.—C. S. Lewis

119. Wherever God erects a house of prayer,
The devil always builds a chapel there;
And 'twill be found, upon examination,
The latter has the largest congregation.
—Daniel Defoe

120. I believe in God in His wisdom and benevolence, and I cannot conceive that such a Being could make such

a species as the human merely to live and die on this earth. If I did not believe (in) a future state, I should believe in no God.—John Adams

121. Seek truth in all things. God reveals Himself through the created world.—Thomas Aquinas

Grace

122. The will of God will not take you where the grace of God cannot keep you.—Author Unknown

123. You say grace before meals. All right. But I say grace before the concert and the opera, and grace before the play and pantomime, and grace before I open a book, and grace before sketching, painting, swimming, fencing, boxing, walking, playing, dancing and grace before I dip the pen in the ink. —G. K. Chesterton

124. God appoints our graces to be nurses to other men's weakness.—Henry Ward Beecher

Heaven

125. Heaven goes by favor. If it went by merit, you would stay out and your dog would go in.—Mark Twain

Holiness

126. A true love of God must begin with a delight in his holiness.—Jonathan Edwards

127. Nothing can make a man truly great but being truly good, and partaking of God's holiness.—Matthew Henry

128. The serene, silent beauty of a holy life is the most powerful influence in the world, next to the might of the Spirit of God.—Blaise Pascal

Judgment

129. There is no man so good, who, were he to submit all his thoughts and actions to the laws, would not deserve hanging ten times in his life.—Montaigne

Ministry

130. The Christian ministry is the worst of all trades, but the best of all professions.—John Newton

Peace

131. Peace is not the absence of conflict, but the presence of God no matter what the conflict.—Author Unknown

132. Five great enemies to peace inhabit with us: avarice, ambition, envy, anger, and pride. If those enemies were to be banished, we should infallibly enjoy perpetual peace.—Petrarch

Prayer

133. If you can't pray as you want to, pray as you can. God knows what you mean.—Vance Havner

134. Every time we pray our horizon is altered, our attitude to things is altered, not sometimes but every time, and the amazing thing is that we don't pray more.—Oswald Chambers

135. When you pray for anyone you tend to modify your personal attitude toward him.—Norman Vincent Peale

136. Do not pray for easy lives, pray to be stronger men. Do not pray for tasks equal to your powers, pray for powers equal to your tasks.—Phillips Brooks

137. The less I pray, the harder it gets; the more I pray, the better it goes.—Martin Luther

138. Teach us to pray that we may cause
The enemy to flee,
That we his evil power may bind,
His prisoners to free.—Watchman Nee

139. Don't force your child to pray. Instead, every night set
aside fifteen minutes before his bedtime for reading
and conversation. Show him pictures of Jesus, and tell
him stories of the Savior. Talk to him of the Heavenly
Father. Explain to him that God sends the sun and
rain. Tell him it is God who makes the flowers grow,
and gives us food to eat. Then lead him in prayers of
thanksgiving and prayers asking the Heavenly Father
for guidance and protection.
—Billy Graham

140. Prayer at its best is the expression of the total life, for
all things else being equal, our prayers are only as
powerful as our lives.—A. W. Tozer

141. There are four ways God answers prayer: No, not yet;
No, I love you too much; Yes, I thought you'd never
ask; Yes, and here's more.—Anne Lewis

142. The potency of prayer hath subdued the strength of
fire; it hath bridled the rage of lions, hushed anarchy
to rest, extinguished wars, appeased the elements,
expelled demons, burst the chains of death, expanded
the gates of heaven, assuaged diseases, repelled
frauds, rescued cities from destruction, stayed the
sun in its course, and arrested the progress of the
thunderbolt.—Saint John Chrysostom

143. Dealing in generalities is the death of prayer.
—J. H. Evans

144. In seasons of distress and grief,
My soul has often found relief,

And oft escaped the tempter's snare,
By thy return, sweet hour of prayer.—W. W. Walford

145. All who call on God in true faith, earnestly from the heart, will certainly be heard, and will receive what they have asked and desired.—Martin Luther

146. By prayer we couple the powers of heaven to our helplessness, the powers which can capture strongholds and make the impossible possible.
—O. Hallesby

147. Faith, and hope, and patience and all the strong, beautiful, vital forces of piety are withered and dead in a prayerless life. The life of the individual believer, his personal salvation, and personal Christian graces have their being, bloom, and fruitage in prayer.
—E. M. Bounds

148. Seven days without prayer makes one weak.
—Allen E. Bartlett

149. There come times when I have nothing more to tell God. If I were to continue to pray in words, I would have to repeat what I have already said. At such times it is wonderful to say to God, "May I be in Thy presence, Lord? I have nothing more to say to Thee, but I do love to be in Thy presence."—O. Hallesby

150. See to it, night and day, that you pray for your children. Then you will leave them a great legacy of answers to prayer, which will follow them all the days of their life. Then you may calmly and with a good conscience depart from them, even though you may not leave them a great deal of material wealth.
—O. Hallesby

151. We can do nothing without prayer. All things can be done by importunate prayer. It surmounts or removes

all obstacles, overcomes every resisting force and gains its ends in the face of invincible hindrances.
—E. M. Bounds

152. We cannot all argue, but we can all pray; we cannot all be leaders, but we can all be pleaders; we cannot all be mighty in rhetoric, but we can all be prevalent in prayer. I would sooner see you eloquent with God than with men.—Charles Haddon Spurgeon

153. Prayer does not change God, but it changes him who prays. —Søren Kierkegaard

154. Restraining prayer, we cease to fight;
Prayer keeps the Christian's armor bright;
And Satan trembles when he sees
The weakest saint upon his knees.—William Cowper

155. The Christian on his knees sees more than the Philosopher on tiptoe.—Dwight L. Moody

156. Prayer is a shield to the soul, a sacrifice to God, and a scourge to Satan.—John Bunyan

157. Prayer is the great engine to overthrow and rout my spiritual enemies, the great means to procure the graces of which I stand in hourly need.—John Newton

158. Unless I had the spirit of prayer, I could do nothing.
—Charles G. Finney

159. We look upon prayer as a means of getting things for ourselves; the Bible's idea of prayer is that we may get to know God Himself.—Oswald Chambers

160. I am not so sure I believe in "the power of prayer," but I believe in the power of the Lord who answers prayer.—Donald Grey Barnhouse

161. The value of consistent prayer is not that He will hear us, but that we will hear Him.—William McGill

162. The purpose of prayer is to reveal the presence of God equally present, all the time, in every condition. —Oswald Chambers

163. No one is a firmer believer in the power of prayer than the devil; not that he practices it, but he suffers from it.—Guy H. King

164. God shapes the world by prayer. Prayers are death-less. They outlive the lives of those who uttered them. —E. M. Bounds

165. I have been driven many times to my knees by the overwhelming conviction that I had nowhere else to go. My own wisdom and that of all about me seemed for the day.—Abraham Lincoln

166. Though we cannot by our prayers give God any information, yet we must by our prayers give him honor.—Matthew Henry

167. Some people will say anything except their prayers. —Horace Wyndham

Religion

168. Most people have some sort of religion. At least they know which church they're staying away from. —John Erskine

169. Some would divorce morality from religion; but religion is the root without which morality would die. —Cyrus Augustus Bartol

170. Men will wrangle for religion, write for it, fight for it, die for it, anything but live for it.—C. C. Colton

Repentance

171. True repentance is to cease from sinning. —Ambrose of Milan

172. Repentance is a hearty sorrow for our past misdeeds, and is a sincere resolution and endeavor, to the utmost of our power, to conform all our actions to the law of God. It does not consist in one single act of sorrow, but in doing works meet for repentance; in a sincere obedience to the law of Christ for the remainder of our lives.—John Locke

173. True repentance always involves reform. —Hosea Ballou

Revival

174. I have long believed there was a divine plan that placed this land here to be found by people of a special kind, that we have a rendezvous with destiny. Yes, there is a spirit moving in this land and a hunger in the people for a spiritual revival. If the task I seek should be given to me, I would pray only that I could perform it in a way that would serve God.—Ronald Reagan

Saints

175. Saints are not formed in great crisis but in the ordinary grind of daily life.—Author Unknown

Scripture

176. Nobody ever outgrows Scripture; the book widens and deepens with our years. —Charles Haddon Spurgeon

Sermon on the Mount

177. We have grasped the mystery of the atom and rejected the Sermon on the Mount.—General Omar Bradley

Sin

178. One leak will sink a ship, and one sin will destroy a
     sinner.—John Bunyan

179. Sin is first pleasing, then it grows easy, then delight-
     ful, then frequent, then habitual, then confirmed; then
     the man is impenitent, then he is obstinate, then he is
     resolved never to repent, and then he is ruined.
     —Robert Leighton

180. Every sin is the result of a collaboration.
     —Stephen Crane

181. There is no sin without previous preparation.
     —Author Unknown

182. Sin has always been an ugly word, but it has been
     made so in a new sense over the last half-century. It
     has been made not only ugly but passé. People are no
     longer sinful, they are only immature or underprivi-
     leged or frightened or, more particularly, sick.
     —Phyllis McGinley

183. Commit the oldest sins the newest kind of ways.
     —William Shakespeare

184. Men are punished by their sins, not for them.
     —Elbert Hubbard

Spiritual Darkness

185. Man is stumbling blindly through a spiritual dark-
     ness while toying with the precarious secrets of life
     and death. The world has achieved brilliance without
     wisdom, power without conscience. We know more
     about war than we know about peace, more about
     killing than we know about living.—General Omar
     Bradley

Temptation

186. Temptation is a part of life. No one is immune—at any age. For temptation is present wherever there is a choice to be made, not only between good and evil, but also between a higher and lower good. For some, it may be a temptation to misuse their gifts, to seek a worthy aim by unworthy means, to lower their ideal to win favor with the electorate, or with their companions and associates.—Ernest Trice Thompson

187. Some temptations come to the industrious, but all temptations attack the idle.—Charles Haddon Spurgeon

188. Keep yourself from opportunity, and God will keep you from sins.—Jacob Cats

Will of God

189. I find doing the will of God leaves me no time for disputing about his plans.—The Marquis of Lossie

LIST #51
101 Q & A of Heavenly Humor

While much of the Bible is serious and meant to be applied to our everyday lives, it's also refreshing for Christians to laugh and have fun. Read on!

1. *Question: What was the name of Isaiah's horse?*
   Answer: Is Me. Isaiah said, "Woe is me."

2. *Question: Who was the first man in the Bible to know the meaning of rib roast?*
   Answer: Adam.

3. *Question: Where does it talk about Honda cars in the Bible?*
   Answer: In Acts 1:14—"These all continued with one accord."

4. *Question: Who was the smallest man in the Bible?*
   Answer: Some people believe that it was Zacchaeus. Others believe it was Nehemiah [Ne-high-a-miah], or Bildad, the Shuhite [Shoe-height]. But in reality it was Peter the disciple. He slept on his watch.

5. *Question: Where in the Bible does it say that we should not play with marbles?*
   Answer: In John 3:7—Jesus said to Nicodemus, "Marvel not . . ." [Marble-Not].

6. *Question: How were Adam and Eve prevented from gambling?*
   Answer: Their paradise [pair-o-dice] was taken away from them.

7. *Question: Where does it say in the Bible that we should not fly in airplanes?*
Answer: In Matthew 28:20—"Lo [Low], I am with you always." Not up high in the air.

8. *Question: What did Noah say while he was loading all the animals on the ark?*
Answer: "Now I herd everything."

9. *Question: When did Moses sleep with five people in one bed?*
Answer: When he slept with his forefathers.

10. *Question: Where in the Bible does it talk about smoking?*
Answer: In Genesis 24:64—Rebekah lighted off her camel.

11. *Question: What was the first theatrical event in the Bible?*
Answer: Eve's appearance for Adam's benefit.

12. *Question: Where in the Bible does it say that fathers should let their sons use the automobile?*
Answer: In Proverbs 13:24—"He that spareth his rod hateth his son."

13. *Question: Why are there so few men with whiskers in heaven?*
Answer: Because most men get in by a close shave.

14. *Question: Who was the best financier in the Bible?*
Answer: Noah. He floated his stock while the whole world was in liquidation.

15. *Question: What simple affliction brought about the death of Samson?*
Answer: Fallen arches.

16. *Question: What did Adam and Eve do when they were expelled from the Garden of Eden?*

Answer: They raised Cain.

17. *Question: What are two of the smallest insects mentioned in the Bible?*
Answer: The widow's "mite," and the "wicked flee"—Mark 12:42 and Proverbs 28:1.

18. *Question: In what place did the cock crow when all the world could hear him?*
Answer: On Noah's ark.

19. *Question: What were the Phoenicians famous for?*
Answer: Blinds.

20. *Question: Where was deviled ham mentioned in the Bible?*
Answer: When the evil spirits entered the swine.

21. *Question: Who introduced the first walking stick?*
Answer: Eve . . . when she presented Adam a little Cain.

22. *Question: Where is medicine first mentioned in the Bible?*
Answer: Where the Lord gives Moses two tablets.

23. *Question: Where in the Bible does it suggest that men should wash dishes?*
Answer: In 2 Kings 21:13—"And I will wipe Jerusalem as a man wipeth a dish, wiping it, and turning it upside down."

24. *Question: Where did Noah strike the first nail in the ark?*
Answer: On the head.

25. *Question: Why was Moses the most wicked man in the Bible?*
Answer: Because he broke the Ten Commandments all at once.

26. *Question: What man in the Bible spoke when he was a very small baby?*
Answer: Job. He cursed the day he was born.

27. *Question: At what time of day was Adam born?*
Answer: A little before Eve.

28. *Question: What man in the Bible had no parents?*
Answer: Joshua, the son of Nun.

29. *Question: Where is tennis mentioned in the Bible?*
Answer: When Joseph served in Pharaoh's court.

30. *Question: Was there any money on Noah's ark?*
Answer: Yes, the duck took a bill, the frog took a greenback, and the skunk took a scent.

31. *Question: Paul the apostle was a great preacher and teacher and earned his living as a tentmaker. What other occupation did Paul have?*
Answer: He was a baker. We know this because he went to Philippi [Fill-a-pie].

32. *Question: Why was Adam's first day the longest?*
Answer: Because it had no Eve.

33. *Question: Why was the woman in the Bible turned into a pillar of salt?*
Answer: Because she was dissatisfied with her Lot.

34. *Question: What is the story in the Bible that talks about a very lazy man?*
Answer: The story about the fellow that loafs and fishes.

35. *Question: Why didn't the last dove return to the ark?*
Answer: Because she had sufficient grounds to stay away.

36. *Question: Who was the most successful physician in the Bible?*
Answer: Job. He had the most patience [patients].

37. *Question: How do we know they used arithmetic in early Bible times?*
Answer: Because the Lord said to multiply on the face of the earth.

38. *Question: How long a period of time did Cain hate his brother?*
Answer: As long as he was Abel.

39. *Question: Who was the first electrician in the Bible?*
Answer: Noah, when he took his family and the animals out of the ark. It made the ark light [arc light].

40. *Question: Who sounded the first bell in the Bible?*
Answer: Cain when he hit Abel.

41. *Question: How did Jonah feel when the great fish swallowed him?*
Answer: Down in the mouth.

42. *Question: Why is a pair of roller skates like the forbidden fruit in the Garden of Eden?*
Answer: They both come before the Fall.

43. *Question: What does the story of Jonah and the great fish teach us?*
Answer: You can't keep a good man down.

44. *Question: Do you know how you can tell that David was older than Goliath?*
Answer: Because David rocked Goliath to sleep.

45. *Question: What is the difference between Noah's ark and an archbishop?*
Answer: One is a high ark, but the other is a hierarch.

46. *Question: When did Ruth treat Boaz badly?*
Answer: When she pulled his ears and trod on his corn.

47. *Question: Where was Solomon's temple located?*
Answer: On the side of his head.

48. *Question: Who is the fastest runner in the world?*
Answer: Adam, because he was first in the human race.

49. *Question: If Moses were alive today, why would he be considered a remarkable man?*
Answer: Because he would be several thousand years old.

50. *Question: How do we know that Noah had a pig in the ark?*
Answer: Because he had Ham.

51. *Question: Why did Moses cross the Red Sea?*
Answer: To avoid Egyptian traffic.

52. *Question: Who was the most popular actor in the Bible?*
Answer: Samson. He brought the house down.

53. *Question: Who was the most ambitious man in the Bible?*
Answer: Jonah, because even the great fish couldn't keep him down.

54. *Question: Who were the twin boys in the Bible?*
Answer: First and Second Samuel.

55. *Question: Where was baseball mentioned in the Bible?*
Answer: Genesis 1:1—In the beginning [big inning].
Genesis 24:15–16—Rebekah went to the well with a "pitcher."
Luke 15:11–32—The prodigal son made a home run.
Judges 7—When Gideon rattled the pitchers.
Exodus 4:4—"And he put forth his hand, and caught it."
Numbers 11:32—"Ten homers."
Psalm 19:12—Who can understand my errors?
Proverbs 18:10—"The righteous runneth into it, and is safe."

Ezekiel 36:12—"Yea, I will cause men to walk."

56. *Question: Who was the first person in the Bible to eat herself out of house and home?*
Answer: Eve

57. *Question: Why was Job always cold in bed?*
Answer: Because he had such miserable comforters.

58. *Question: How were the Egyptians paid for goods taken by the Israelites when they fled from Egypt?*
Answer: The Egyptians got a check on the bank of the Red Sea.

59. *Question: Why didn't they play cards on Noah's ark?*
Answer: Because Noah sat on the deck.

60. *Question: In the story of the Good Samaritan, why did the Levite pass by on the other side?*
Answer: Because the poor man had already been robbed.

61. *Question: Who was the straightest man in the Bible?*
Answer: Joseph. Pharaoh made a ruler out of him.

62. *Question: Which came first—the chicken or the egg?*
Answer: The chicken, of course. God doesn't lay any eggs.

63. *Question: When is high finance first mentioned in the Bible?*
Answer: When Pharaoh's daughter took a little prophet [profit] from the bulrushes.

64. *Question: What is the only wage that does not have any deductions?*
Answer: The wages of sin.

65. *Question: At what season of the year did Eve eat the fruit?*
Answer: Early in the Fall.

66. *Question: If Methuselah was the oldest man in the Bible [969 years of age], why did he die before his father?*
Answer: His father was Enoch. Enoch never died, he was translated.

67. *Question: What has God never seen, Abraham Lincoln seldom saw, and we see every day?*
Answer: Isaiah 40:25; 46:5—"To whom then will ye liken me, or shall I be equal? Saith the Holy One." God has never seen his equal. Abraham Lincoln seldom saw his equal, and we see our equals every day.

68. *Question: On the ark, Noah probably got milk from the cows. What did he get from the ducks?*
Answer: Quackers.

69. *Question: One of the first things Cain did after he left the Garden of Eden was to take a nap. How do we know this?*
Answer: Because he went to the land of Nod—Genesis 4:16

70. *Question: Where do you think the Israelites may have deposited their money?*
Answer: At the banks of the Jordan.

71. *Question: Why do you think that the kangaroo was the most miserable animal on the ark?*
Answer: Because her children had to play inside during the rain.

72. *Question: What prophet in the Bible was a space traveler?*
Answer: Elijah. He went up in a fiery chariot.

73. *Question: What do you have that Cain, Abel, and Seth never had?*

241

Answer: Grandparents.

74. *Question: What city in the Bible was named after something that you find on every modern-day car?*
Answer: Tyre [tire].

75. *Question: When the ark landed on Mount Ararat, was Noah the first one out?*
Answer: No, he came fourth out of the ark.

76. *Question: What was the difference between the 10,000 soldiers of Israel and the 300 soldiers Gideon chose for battle?*
Answer: 9,700.

77. *Question: Where is the first math problem mentioned in the Bible?*
Answer: When God divided the light from the darkness.

78. *Question: Why did Noah have to punish and discipline the chickens on the ark?*
Answer: Because they were using "fowl" language.

79. *Question: What was the most expensive meal served in the Bible, and who ate it?*
Answer: Lentils. Esau ate it, and it cost him his birthright.

80. *Question: Certain days in the Bible passed by more quickly than most of the days. Which days were these?*
Answer: The fast days.

81. *Question: Matthew and Mark have something that is not found in Luke and John. What is it?*
Answer: The letter "a."

82. *Question: Which one of Noah's sons was considered to be a clown?*

Answer: His second son. He was always a Ham.

83. *Question: What was the first game mentioned in the Bible?*
Answer: When Adam and Eve played hide-and-seek with God.

84. *Question: What made Abraham so smart?*
Answer: He knew a Lot.

85. *Question: What is most of the time black, sometimes brown or white, but should be red?*
Answer: The Bible.

86. *Question: Why did everyone on the ark think that horses were pessimistic?*
Answer: Because they always said neigh.

87. *Question: Who was the first person in the Bible to have surgery performed on him?*
Answer: Adam, when God removed one of his ribs.

88. *Question: When was the Red Sea very angry?*
Answer: When the children of Israel crossed it.

89. *Question: What vegetable did Noah not want on the ark?*
Answer: Leeks.

90. *Question: Why do you think Jonah could not trust the ocean?*
Answer: He knew that there was something fishy in it.

91. *Question: How do we know that God has a sense of humor?*
Answer: Because He can take a "rib."

92. *Question: What time was it when the hippopotamus sat on Noah's rocking chair?*
Answer: Time to get a new chair.

93. *Question: What does God both give away and keep at the same time?*
Answer: His promises.

94. *Question: During the six days of creation, which weighed more—the day or the night?*
Answer: The night, because the day was light.

95. *Question: What did the skunks on the ark have that no other animals had?*
Answer: Baby skunks.

96. *Question: What type of tea does the Bible suggest that we not drink?*
Answer: Vanity [vani-tea].

97. *Question: In what book of the Bible do we find something that is in modern-day courtrooms?*
Answer: Judges.

98. *Question: Which animal on the ark was the rudest?*
Answer: The mockingbird.

99. *Question: What kind of soap did God use to keep the oceans clean?*
Answer: Tide.

100. *Question: How do we know that the disciples were very cruel to the corn?*
Answer: Because they pulled its ears.

101. *Question: How many animals could Noah put into the empty ark?*
Answer: One. After that the ark would not be empty.